The Complete Home Video Director

The Complete Home Video Director

BY

DAVID OWEN

foulsham
London • New York • Toronto • Sydney

foulsham
Yeovil Road, Slough, Berkshire SL1 4JH

ISBN 0-572-01784-7
Copyright © 1992 David Owen

Printed in Great Britain by St. Edmundsbury Press, Bury St Edmunds
Phototypeset in Great Britain by Typesetting Solutions, Slough

CONTENTS

INTRODUCTION

Video has become so much a part of our lives that occasionally we find ourselves taken aback by the sheer pace of its development. Britain has long been in the forefront of video usage, with one of the highest percentages of VCR ownership in the world. The idea of borrowing a video copy of a feature film, on a night when the broadcast television programmes offer little in the way of entertainment value, has become as familiar a leisure choice as a visit to the cinema or the pub. The idea of recording a programme off-air, to watch at a more convenient time, or to avoid a clash between two worthwhile attractions on opposing channels, is second nature to more than four viewers out of five. And the latest recorders to reach the market offer features like high quality sound, or the option of recording two different programmes at once, or watching one video while recording another programme off-air — surely the ultimate in flexibility?

But the most significant advances have been in the do-it-yourself part of the video market — the camcorders, and the equipment associated with them, which allow enthusiasts the opportunity to make their own television programmes, with more and more ambitious objectives. In one way, today's equipment makes creative programme production easier than ever — in another, it's made a more demanding and more complex exercise, *because* of the flexibility and the sophistication of the equipment which is now available. But this combination means that it's now more worthwhile than ever to take the time to understand the medium, and the equipment involved, from the creative point of view — in terms of what it can do, and how to control it, rather than how it actually works.

That's the purpose of this book — to look beyond the individual details of each particular item of

7

hardware, at the ideas and methods which can help to build up a professional, original and individual programme, with the minimum of disappointment. It's a skill which is worth the learning. The combination of moving pictures in colour, with automatically synchronised sound and instant replay, means that video has no rival when it comes to recording and preserving a slice of reality — to be played back whenever you, and your audience, want.

It's true to say there's no real difficulty in learning to operate today's video equipment. More and more functions are being made automatic or semi-automatic, leaving the user to concentrate on the purely creative business of shooting and recording what he wants. But there *are* still lessons which are worth learning. The do's and don'ts of making an entertaining film which is interesting to watch, apply with just as much force to making video programmes. Lighting your subject, framing your shots properly, telling the story through the accepted grammar of movie-making — all are essential in the making of a home video which looks and sounds thoroughly professional.

Today's equipment is capable of delivering better and better pictures in terms of sharpness and realism — so it's now worthwhile, more than ever, to learn how to be a professional director, producer, cameraman, sound recordist, and editor. Today's video cameras and recorders really do offer amazing value for money. For a few hundred pounds apiece, you can buy equipment which does just the same job as a professional, broadcast-quality camera or recorder costing ten or even a hundred times as much. There are differences, of course. The kit used by television companies is more complex because it either uses a wider tape format, or the tape runs at a higher speed so that there's a larger area of tape on which the picture information is stored. There are all kinds of circuits and features designed to enhance picture quality and improve sharpness, to cope with low light levels and high-contrast subjects, and a hundred and one other things.

But at the end of the day, the home-video enthusiast with his camcorder will be looking for the same qualities in his shots as the professional TV camera-man — or he should be. The fact that the picture quality will be slightly less sharp with the cheaper camera, though this gap is narrowing year by year, matters less than the fact that the pictures you shoot really will be your own: unique, a part of your own life and your own inspiration in a way that even the best broadcast television programme can never be. In short, making your own video is a genuinely active and creative pastime, in contrast to the purely passive role of watching other people's programmes on your television set.

The nuts and bolts of creative programme-making will be covered throughout the rest of this book. This introduction deals with the first steps — coming to terms with operating the equipment you have. Only when the knowledge of which buttons to press and which adjustments to make become second nature can you really feel free to tackle the subject of your programme, and develop a treat-ment and an approach which will do it justice. It's directly equivalent to the position of the learner driver, forced to learn how to master steering and gear-changing, and the use of the clutch, the accelerator and the brake pedal, before being able to move on to the sheer freedom and enjoyment of driving a car.

Many readers will have progressed beyond the L-plates stage of camcorder operation. If so, then please skip this opening section, and move straight on to the chapters dealing with how to *use* the equipment as opposed to how to operate it. For those who are new to present-day camcorders, either because this is their first introduction to video programme-making, or because they hope to trade in an older camera/recorder for one of today's infinitely more ambitious models, then it will do no harm to review the kind of controls and options which present-day equipment carries. So here goes . . .

CHOOSING YOUR CAMCORDER

The first point to remember is that, while all video cameras and camcorders work in basically the same way, there are several different formats and designs on the market. In fact, if you look at the market beyond Britain, you'll find that, because different

1	External microphone jack (MIC)	35	Date/time on/off button
2	Exclusive microphone	36	Recording time reset button
3	Zoom lens	37	Date/time mode button
4	Auto-focus sensor window	38	Viewfinder mount
5	White balance sensor window	39	Page button
6	Electronic viewfinder	40	Title on/off button
7	Full auto button	41	Manual zoom lever
8	Focus select button	42	Macro button
9	Shutter select button	43	Manual focus ring
10	White balance select button	44	Lens hood
11	Counter memory button	45	Recording time on/off switch
12	Liquid crystal display (LCD)	46	Date/time select button
13	Counter reset button	47	Date/time set button
14	Cassette holder	48	Viewfinder cable connector
15	Power switch	49	Power zoom buttons
16	Recording standby button	50	Image reverse button
17	Monitor button	51	Title memory button
18	Quick review/edit button	52	Colour button
19	Rewind/shuttle search button	53	Lens cap
20	Play button	54	Dioptric adjustment control
21	Fast forward/shuttle search button	55	Slots for shoulder strap
22	Pause/still button	56	Tracking control
23	Stop button	57	DC In terminal
24	Eject switch	58	Grip strap
25	Standard play/long play recording mode select switch	59	Battery mount
26	Dubbing on/off switch	60	Lens cap hook
27	Remote control jack	61	Battery pack release lever
28	Earphone jack	62	Video Out Switch
29	AV connector	63	S-VHS switch
30	S-video out connector	64	Tripod mounting socket
31	Alarm on/off switch	65	Stud hole
32	Thumb rest	66	Clock battery compartment
33	Recording start/stop button	67	Back light compensation button
34	Second recording start/stop button	68	Fader button

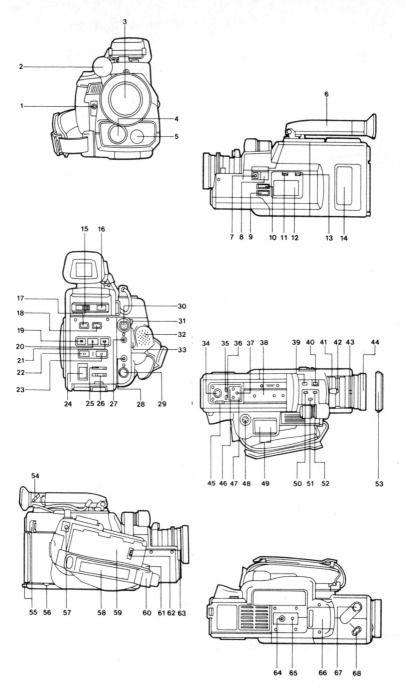

Figure 1. Modern camcorders pack a long list of features into a very small space. The key opposite reveals the level of sophistication on a current JVC model.

countries use different systems for transmitting and receiving colour television pictures — NTSC in the USA and Canada, SECAM in France, PAL in Britain and Germany, and so on — these differences are reflected in the camcorders and VCRs sold on each market. So don't, for example, buy a camcorder in the USA unless you expect to play back its pictures in the USA. If you're going on holiday in North America, and you want to bring your videotapes back with you for playback at home, it's better to take your UK camcorder with you. Then at least the TV systems you shoot on, and play back on, will be the same.

In all these cases, though, the camcorder does the same job. Its role is essentially the same as that of a movie camera — or for that matter the more familiar kind of camera for taking still snapshots. It uses its lens to focus an image of the object at which it's pointed. But instead of focusing this image onto a film where it can be recorded chemically, it focuses it onto a screen where the different parts of the picture are transformed into electrical signals.

These electrical signals are passed to the recorder, which then records them onto the magnetic tape in the video cassette, in exactly the same way as sound signals can be recorded onto magnetic tape in an audio tape recorder or cassette recorder. Once the recording is finished, the videotape cassette can be played back on any recorder. The signals obtained from the original picture will then re-create that picture on the television screen — rather as the signals from a broadcast television transmitter are received by a television aerial and fed down a cable to the set to be reassembled into a picture.

This gives video its two most obvious advantages over film as a medium for recording moving pictures. First, because the picture information is recorded onto the videotape magnetically, it's available for instant replay at any time. That means you can see what a shot looks like while there's still time to reshoot it if need be; waiting for cine film to be developed and processed could take days or even weeks. Second, the magnetic tape is completely reusable. This means if the shot isn't quite as you wanted it, you can not only reshoot it straight away, but you can record it over the same part of the tape, so that you only take home the material you're completely happy with.

That apart, the system on which your particular camcorder records will vary too. This is a combination of the cassettes which are used to record what is being shot and the circuitry which governs the recording and playback. So far as the cassettes are concerned, modern camcorders operate on two different widths of tape — the half-inch tape used in domestic VHS-format video recorders, and the narrower eight-millimetre tapes used in the Video 8 format. Camcorders using half-inch tapes — in conjunction either with the normal VHS system, or the enhanced S-VHS version which uses a higher frequency carrier wave to provide a sharper picture — actually use a smaller VHS-C cassette than the mains VHS machines, but these can be played back in an ordinary VHS machine by placing the camera cassette in a special adaptor, which is then loaded into the mains machine proper.

Eight-millimetre tapes can also be found in two closely similar varieties — for the basic Video 8 system, and the enhanced-quality Hi8 system which uses more sophisticated circuitry to record more picture information on the tape. This means sharper pictures and other benefits we shall explain later — but it also means having to use tapes which, though they're the same size as ordinary Video 8 tapes, are rather more expensive. For the time being, the drawback of the eight-millimetre system compared with VHS-C is that the tapes can't be played back on an ordinary VHS recorder without copying them onto VHS first, though they can be viewed by linking the camcorder directly to the TV. But as the choice of Video 8 mains recorders and pre-recorded feature-film cassettes widens, the percentage of people who use this format for home video is increasing.

So far as operating the camcorder is concerned, however, there's virtually no difference between the two systems — it's merely a matter of making the best choice to suit your existing equipment, or bearing in mind the way you intend building up your programme-making kit (more on that later). And, of course, ensuring that you buy, and use, the right cassettes to suit your machine.

Until recently today's cameras were based on the shoulder-mounted cameras used by professional television cameramen when out on location, where portability is important. Known in the trade as the 'Iron Parrot', the shoulder-mounted camera has two advantages. It's less tiring to use, even with the larger and heavier professional cameras, and it's easier to obtain steady shots when a tripod isn't available, or when there's no time to set one up. Because they are still smaller and lighter than their predecessors, the latest camera/recorders have reverted back to the hand-held design, similar to the small home-movie cine cameras which were popular before the video revolution. Like them, they need careful handling because they are so light — check the instructions in the owner's manual about the right way to hold them and reach all the controls, most of which can be operated by one hand. But always use your other hand to help steady the camera whilst making any other adjustments, like changing the focus, otherwise it is all too easy for camera shake to mar your carefully-planned shots without you realising it until afterwards. We'll look at this in more detail later.

FEATURES, CONTROLS — AND PRECAUTIONS

You'll notice straight away some very obvious differences from a typical home-movie cine camera. The lens system will look much the same, but instead of an optical viewfinder, your video camera will have an electronic viewfinder: basically a very small black-and-white TV set which shows you exactly the picture the lens will be recording, with only the colour missing. There will also be a set of

14

buttons on a control panel which look after various camera functions. For example, one of them will control the focusing arrangements, to adjust the lens to produce a sharp picture, depending on the distance between you and the subject. Many of today's video cameras have an automatic focus facility. All you have to do is sight the camera so that the subject you want to shoot is seen against a ring marking at the centre of the screen, and it will focus automatically.

There are times when this can be useful — as when following an object which is approaching you or receding from you, without the need to readjust the focus manually to take this into account. But in most cases, you'll need the extra control you have by setting the focus manually. Turning the focus adjustment ring on the lens barrel gives you a greater degree of control when you're shooting — but first you'll need to select 'manual' on the focus-mode control on the side of the camera.

It's also important to remember that when you want to fit a filter or a special-effects lens to the front of the existing lens system (more on this later too), you must switch from 'auto-focus' to 'manual'. In most cases, the automatic focus won't work when extra lens combinations are being used, and leaving the automatic function on while they're being fitted can result in damage.

There are other sensible precautions worth bearing in mind when looking after a camcorder. Some of them are obvious enough — protecting the unit from shocks, vibration or strong magnetic fields. In fact, replacing the tubes which were used in the first video cameras with today's charge-coupled-device (CCD) chips and circuits has made them much more robust, as well as producing much better pictures. But it's still sensible to treat them carefully — and some hazards are rather less obvious. Heat, for example. Keeping a camcorder in high temperatures — like on the seat of a car with the windows closed on a hot summer's day — can cause damage to the CCD and the autofocus sensors, and if really hot, to the casing of the camera itself. Even using the camcorder in high temperatures, or in freezing and sub-zero conditions, isn't recommended.

Letting the camera point at the sun, with the lens aperture open, was a sure way to leave a permanent trace on the tubes. Even CCD cameras are vulnerable to strong light sources so, when in doubt, check the lens cap is on — *except* when you want to shoot! The same precautions hold good for viewfinder eyepieces too.

But a more unexpected hazard is moisture. Obviously, getting the camera wet is as much to be avoided as with any other piece of electrical equipment — though most manufacturers offer rain hoods for shooting in bad weather, or even fully waterproof casings for shooting underwater. But condensation is a much more insidious threat, so that most camcorders have a moisture warning to alert the user to dampness within the system. In some cases, the unit simply won't work until the components dry out, so it's impossible to ignore. Usually, the problem arises when the camcorder is taken from a cold place into a warmer one — or it's being used in a cold place where the heating has just been put on, you're shooting near the outlet from an air conditioner, or in extremely humid conditions.

It's also important to understand that camcorders shouldn't be left in the 'pause' mode for too long. There are two reasons for this. The tape and the recording heads may become damaged, and the batteries will run out that much faster. So most cameras have a safety device which automatically puts them in 'stop' mode if they're left in 'pause' for more than a few minutes. The tape will be unlaced from the recording heads, and the picture will disappear from the viewfinder. If you find this has happened, when you want to record another shot, all you have to do is press the 'standby' button, and the picture will reappear in the viewfinder. Then you can select and frame a subject, and press the 'start' button to begin recording the next shot. Should you want to check what you've just been shooting there's usually a 'review' button which you can press, and the recorder will replay (through the viewfinder) the last two or three seconds of the previous shot.

If you want to play back any more of the recorded picture, you can use the normal 'rewind' and 'play' buttons on the recorder panel of your camera. But you will then need to switch back to the camera controls before shooting again. Normally in a video camera the iris — the aperture of the lens which controls the amount of light entering the camera — operates automatically, which does at least save you the trouble of readjusting the lens aperture ring as the light level changes. But there is usually an override button which lets you shoot objects against a fairly bright background, which would otherwise render them as silhouettes. This is called a backlight compensator, and when it's disengaged the camera reverts to automatic-iris operating.

There's one other iris adjustment which is becoming increasingly common, and that's the 'fade' button. When this is pressed, it closes the iris down so that less and less light comes in through the lens, until the light is cut off. The effect of this on the picture is to cause it to go darker and darker, until it eventually fades out completely to a black screen. Since a clever circuit fades the sound level down in keeping with the picture, this makes it a convenient device for ending a sequence, or a programme. Pressing the button again, when the lens aperture has been closed, allows the opposite process to take place. The picture fades up from a black screen, with the sound level rising as well. You can use this effect deliberately, to begin a programme, or you'll see later how a fade-out/fade-up in quick succession can be used as an effect which allows you to bridge a jump in location, or suggest the passing of time.

Finally, on most of today's cameras you'll find another invaluable lens adjustment: the zoom. This allows you to readjust the lens so that you can change the field of view of the camera. In other words, if you focus on a particular subject such as a boat on a lake, you have the choice of a wide shot which shows the boat as a small object in the distance with the lake and the surrounding country-side in the frame too. Or you can zoom in to show the boat in close-up almost filling the frame, with just the water around it and none of the wider surroundings in the shot. Between these two extremes, you can frame the picture anywhere you like by adjusting the zoom, and you can actually zoom in and out as part of the shot itself. Some cameras have manual zoom adjustment, where you can zoom in and out by turning another ring on the lens barrel — but most now tend to have a power zoom, driven by an electric motor and controlled by a rocker switch to move in and out at will, with the pressure on the switch determining the speed of the zoom. Next come the controls which determine the way in which the picture seen through the lens is turned into the electrical signals sent to the video recorder part of the combination.

Figure 2. Zooming in can take you from a distant view of a subject (above left) to a closer view (above right), without moving the camera position.

The most important of these is the 'white-balance' control. This adjusts the camcorder's responses to the colours of the objects being shot, depending on the kind of light in which they're seen. For example, full daylight has a slightly bluish cast, while domestic tungsten-filament lighting displays a more yellow quality. When shooting early in the morning or late in the evening, there tends to be a reddening of the light long before this becomes perceptible to the human eye, since our optical system tends to compensate for these variations quite automatically. But for lifelike pictures through the camcorder, the variations in the temperature, and therefore the colour, of the light, need to be taken into account, which means adjusting the camcorder's colour balance to suit the conditions at the time and place of the shoot.

The result being aimed for is that a white object will appear white when seen on the screen, because the main colours which make up white light are in perfect balance — hence the term 'white balance'. For professional cameras used on location, this usually means holding up a pure white card in front of the lens, and pressing a button to initiate the camera's own circuits to carry out the adjustment automatically. When the camera is then used in different conditions out comes the card again and the process is repeated, but this time the camera is readjusted to the new lighting conditions which exist at the time.

With some camcorders, the process is a great deal simpler. All you have to do is select one of the three most common sets of lighting conditions — daylight, tungsten or halogen lighting, and fluorescent lighting, and the camera does the rest. Or, on most models, you can select an automatic white-balance mode, and the camera will sense the current lighting temperature and make the balancing adjustments itself quite automatically.

Most camcorders also have a 'shutter-select' control. Essentially, video cameras work in the same way as cine cameras in that they record the action frame by frame, controlled by a shutter which allows the image to reach the recording medium (film or videotape) long enough for a single still picture to be captured. Usually this is one-fiftieth of a second (since a video camera on the UK's PAL TV system records twenty-five frames per second, and each frame is made up of two fields). But when covering high-speed (particularly sports) subjects in bright lighting conditions, it may be desirable to shoot with a faster shutter such as 1/125 second, 1/500 second or even 1/1000 second, for better results on slow motion or still replay.

The camera will also have a facility which allows you to record a new shot at whatever point on the preceding shot you want to add it — in what is called an 'assemble edit'. Assuming that the camcorder has been turned off since you took the previous shot, this means that you have to switch the system on to 'play', wait five seconds for the tape to thread itself around the heads and for a picture to appear in the viewfinder. Then you wait till you reach the point at which you want the new shot to begin, and press the 'pause' button. From that point, everything is set up for the new shot.

When you're ready to record, all you need do is press the 'record' button, followed by the 'start' button and the new shot will begin recording at the right point on the tape, with a smooth edit which allows you to build up a complete programme shot by shot. It also allows you to go back to record a shot over an unsatisfactory attempt at the same shot. So, by carefully reviewing what you've recorded (subject to the battery life you have left, which will be displayed inside the viewfinder) you can make sure that the programme material you build up is as good as time and trouble will allow. When you've finished, save batteries by going into 'standby' and then switch off.

The latest, more sophisticated camcorders have one valuable extra feature, which alters the whole basis on which programmes can be planned and shot, and which is covered in greater detail later in this book. Essentially, it's the facility which allows them to be used, with a mains VCR and an edit controller, as part of a full edit suite to build up the finished programme, just as the professionals do, from shots which may have been recorded in a totally different order from that in which they appear in the finished programme. This is without doubt the most valuable option of all in terms of producing original and entertaining programmes, as will become clear when we look more closely at the steps involved.

YOUR FIRST SHOOT

For the time being, however, let's take the first simple steps towards making a programme, by practising the art of using the camcorder. First of all, make sure the cassette has been loaded and the battery power has been switched on. Check the white balance has been adjusted according to the lighting conditions in which you're shooting, check the focus has been set to manual and press the buttons to put the camera into the recording-standby mode. This will lace up the tape around the recording heads, and switch the picture seen through the lens onto the screen of the viewfinder.

It's essential to master the art of holding the camcorder correctly. In most cases, camcorders are now so light and compact that they don't need to be carried on the shoulder like the larger and heavier professional cameras. The layout of the controls and buttons, from the recording start/stop button to the rocker switch for the power zoom, virtually dictates how the camcorder fits into the hand, but the difficult part is learning to hold it still. A heavy camera on the shoulder is easier to steady, even though it's much more fatiguing to use, so a camcorder operator has to practise the rather different art of combining a steady grip with very slow, smooth and even movements where these are necessary to record the right shots, or to cope with movements imposed from outside. For example, when shooting from a moving car or train, or when standing in the wind, the priority must be to isolate the camera as far as possible from shocks or vibration, by cushioning it with the arms and keeping the legs as well-balanced as possible.

Figure 3. The right way to hold a camcorder — using your body to support it and steady it while still being able to reach all the controls with both hands.

It may help to bear two points in mind. When you play back your pictures for the first time, you'll probably be disappointed by how unsteady they look. When we look at a scene with the human eye, we're not aware of the movements we make, or of the shocks we're subjected to, because of whatever we may be sitting or standing on. An observer standing on the deck of a boat in a rough sea and looking at the horizon will see it apparently perfectly steady, because the brain's optical processing circuits can compensate for the unwanted movements of the eyes. Some camcorders have special steadying buttons which can carry out much the same function in damping out steady vibrations, though even these may find it difficult to cope with sudden unexpected movements.

The difference between the picture seen by the eye, and that seen through the camera lens and played back on the screen, is that the image seen on the screen preserves every shake and movement of the camera, and beyond a certain level these can be extremely distracting. So always remember to hold the camera as steadily as you possibly can, and only move it slowly and evenly from subject to subject. It's also worth bearing in mind that every movement is greatly magnified at the end of the zoom, when you're concentrating in close-up on a distant object. Better by far to begin on the wider end of the zoom, when movements aren't so apparent, and use a tripod or your surroundings to provide a steadying influence before trying more ambitious zooms and telephoto shots.

Now let's find a suitable subject. Something far enough away to avoid focus troubles, and static enough to allow you to concentrate on the camera without worrying about your subject walking off in the middle of the shot, would be ideal. Let's say, for example, it's a large and colourful poster on the other side of the road. Point the camera at the

Figure 4. When you first look through the viewfinder, the picture will probably be fuzzy and out of focus (above right). Turn the focus ring until the picture is sharp (above left).

subject, and look at it through the viewfinder. The chances are that it will look fuzzy and out of focus. With your left hand, move the focusing ring until the image appears clear and sharp in the viewfinder.

Now, holding the camera as steadily as you can, press the stop/start button. The camera will now be recording, and you can usually check this in the viewfinder by seeing a 'record' light or LCD symbol illuminate, or begin flashing steadily. On the more sophisticated cameras, there will be other warning lights inside the viewfinder, where you can't miss them however hard you may be concentrating on your shooting — one to warn you that the batteries are getting low, another to tell you the light level is too low for good results, and sometimes another to tell you that you're nearing the end of the tape. We won't concern ourselves with these other lights just now — but you need to watch out for any of these warnings as your shooting proceeds.

Next we'll try using the power zoom. This is operated by the rocker switch mounted on the side of the lens housing by your first and second fingers. Pressing with your index finger pushes down the rearmost half of the rocker switch and causes the lens to zoom out, or appear to pull back away from the subject. Pressing with your second finger on the front half of the switch causes the lens to zoom in, towards the subject. Usually you can operate the start/stop button with your right thumb, pressing once to stop the recording, and pressing again to restart it. This leaves your left hand free to help steady the camera, to change the focus when this is needed (remembering to keep your left hand well clear of the lens), or to press the 'backlight' or 'fade' buttons.

Now press with your second finger on the front half of the rocker switch, and you'll find the subject seems to loom larger and closer in the viewfinder, so that you end up with the centre of your original picture occupying the entire frame. Instead of the whole poster, you'll now be concentrating on just part of it — the slogan, the frame and the background will all be out of the viewfinder image. The chances are this is now out of focus, since the depth of field — that is the distance range over which objects are seen in focus without readjusting the camera lens — is least on the close-up end of the zoom. But if you now refocus, so the image becomes sharp and clear once again, you'll find that by pressing on the rear part of the rocker switch, you can zoom out from the close-up shot, all the way to

Figure 5. Zoom in from the long shot (upper picture) to hold the centre of the picture in close-up (lower picture). Adjust the focus to produce a sharp image. If you then zoom back to the long shot, the picture will remain in focus.

the long shot at the opposite end of the zoom, and the subject will remain in focus throughout. You'll also notice it's a lot easier to hold the camera steady enough for a static picture at this end of the zoom than it was in close-up.

Many cameras also have a 'macro' facility on the lens which allows you to focus on a subject which is much closer than the normal limit of the lens — right up to the lens surface itself in some instances. In this case, you press a special 'macro' button, and then use the manual zoom control to bring your subject into sharp focus. You can even pull back all the way in a normal zoom by moving the manual adjustment right back to the opposite extreme of the range, giving you a longer than normal zoom-out option from an extremely close-range subject.

Whichever way you use it, the zoom is an extremely useful facility. Not only does it allow you to frame a shot exactly as you want it — deciding how much of the subject to include in the picture — without having to move your camera position, it also allows you to link your subjects and their contexts in the programme sequence you may be building up. Let's assume, for example, you wanted to record a shot of a child building a sandcastle on a crowded holiday beach. You could start with the camera fully zoomed out, showing a section of the beach and the crowded sea beyond, with people paddling, sunbathing, reading or running up and down — but by zooming in to hold the close-up shot of a single child absorbed with bucket and spade, you're focusing the attention of your audience exactly where you want it to be concentrated.

Equally, the opposite process — zooming out — can be used to make a different point. Let's say this time that the child is busy building the sandcastle, but it's a question of sheer determination, because the day is so bleak and cold there's no one else brave enough to venture onto the sand. This time, by starting on the child in close-up, you can conceal that fact from your audience. They'll probably assume it's a conventional holiday shot, so that when you zoom out to reveal, as you move back further and further from your subject, that he or she is completely alone on a wide sweep of sand and sea, your shot will have the surprise effect you want it to have. We'll look later at other ideas for ways of using the zoom, but these two examples should show what a powerfully useful, and easily used device it is.

PANNING AND TILTING

Now let's look at one or two other ways of linking subjects in a sequence. Taking our poster as an example, let's imagine you want to follow up your shot of a hoarding which may be advertising airline services, with one of nearby road traffic stopped in a long queue. If you pick your camera position carefully, you can shoot both shots from the same place. You *could* shoot them as separate shots, finishing the first shot and then cutting to the second subject before you start recording again, and often you might well have to do that for all kinds of reasons. But when you can move from one subject to the other in a single shot, it's a neat way of bridging the action and bringing a different kind of flow to the sequence.

First, frame up again on the poster hoarding, without recording. Then, holding the camera as steadily as you can, swing slowly round till the traffic queue is framed in the viewfinder. Try to decide the best compromise you can between the right framing for the opening shot — the poster — and for the closing shot, without changing either the focus or the degree of zoom. If necessary, you may have to move your camera position slightly to produce the right result.

Then frame up again on the start of the shot — the poster board — and start recording. Wait a second or so to establish the shot on the screen, and then start pivoting slowly towards the second subject. When you reach it, try to finish the movement by slowing

27

to a smooth stop, rather than reaching it and stopping with a jerk. When you reach it, hold the shot for a second before you stop recording. Be specially careful not to make the beginner's mistake of overshooting the picture you want to end the shot with, and then moving back in the reverse direction to frame it up properly. If that happens, better to play the shot back in the viewfinder to find the start point, and then record another attempt or 'take' over it.

Figure 6. Three steps in a PAN LEFT, to link two parts of the same scene: from the opening frame of the signal box, past the level crossing to the closing frame showing the two signals.

The name for this shot is a PAN. If you were moving to the right to move from your opening shot to your closing shot, then it would appear in a camera script as a PAN RIGHT. If you were moving in the opposite direction, it would appear as a PAN LEFT. But there's also another way of linking shots, by moving upwards or downwards instead of to left or right. These are described as a PAN UP (or TILT UP) and a PAN DOWN (or TILT DOWN). One example might be to start with a shot of a wedding party entering the church and then pan up to the church clock showing the time. Another shot of the clock showing the time a half-hour or so later, and you can pan down to the party posing in readiness for the photographs to be taken — a neat way of showing the passing of time, and missing out the part of the story you didn't plan to record.

Let's assume that you have been trying out each of these different movements and ideas for yourself, practising first with the camera in standby mode to enable you to see the picture in the viewfinder, and then making a recording. Now we reach the acid test. It's time to take a look at what you've recorded. Depending on the type of camera you have it may or may not be possible to play back the tape and watch the picture in the camera viewfinder. But the best way is to take it back to base and play it back through the television set. This will mean you'll see your pictures in colour, and you'll see them on a large enough screen to show up all the blemishes and imperfections, and you'll save your batteries.

Be prepared for a shock. We all of us tend to spend a good deal of time watching television made by professionals, on very costly equipment, and sparing no effort or expense to produce a smooth and glossy result, from the technical point of view at least. Your picture quality will fall short of that kind of standard, but the fact that it shows your neighbourhood and what you've just been shooting gives it a special kind of immediacy, and a special kind of excitement. Try looking at it objectively, and don't be discouraged at this stage. Look for faults so that you can learn how to correct them later, as your skill and experience improve and you become more professional.

Watch specially for the pans from subject to subject. Unless you have some experience, or have a natural aptitude for this kind of shot — which is most unusual — you'll probably find they don't work too well at first. If you pan too quickly, all you'll tend to have is a confused blur once you move off the first subject, and until you reach the second. To be successful, a pan has to be much slower than you could transfer your gaze from the first object to the second using your own eyes. Second, even if the pace is right, you'll probably find the start and stop of the pan are jerky and distracting. What you must strive for is a smooth transition from the beginning of the shot (where the camera is stationary) into the pan itself, and an equally smooth transition from the end of the pan to the end of the shot where the camera is still once again, this time concentrating on the second subject.

What's needed is actually a very slow acceleration, so that you start off the pan very slowly and build up gradually to the movement to the second subject. In the same way, as you reach the end of the shot, you have to slow down progressively, so that you can stop with the subject perfectly in the frame, without jerking the camera and without overshooting and having to pan back. Those are the hallmarks of the amateur, and they're surprisingly difficult to eliminate. The only answer is practice, so that moving slowly, steadily, and smoothly from shot to shot becomes second nature, a completely automatic response which allows you to concentrate on the subjects which form the beginning and end of the shot.

This is probably even more true of shots which involve tilting up and down, since this requires a more difficult movement. Here again the secret is to try to move yourself and the camera as a combination, rather than simply tilting the camera up and down. Lean backwards from the waist as you tilt up, and bend forwards from the waist as you tilt down — and keep the camera as steady as possible when you do it. Finally, remember that the same speeding up and slowing down process should be applied at the start and end of a zoom shot in either a wide-angle or telephoto direction.

The next step is to try out all these techniques with a variety of different subjects. Rehearse them, record them, and then play them back with a close eye on factors like speed, smoothness and steadiness. At first, you're almost bound to be disappointed. What seems, when you are shooting it, to be a slow movement from subject to subject will seem a jerky, confusing blur when you watch it on the screen without any of the visual cues we can rely on when making the same transition with the unaided eye. The slightest hesitation or variation in speed will seem magnified. The stop and start of the pan will seem jerky and abrupt. But don't be discouraged. Camera movements need skill, a skill which can be learned and practised like any other, and in time you'll find your movements will become relaxed, instinctive and progressively more confident.

This is where the lightness and compactness of the modern camcorders becomes an even more positive advantage. It's worth getting used to taking it with you on a walk in the country, a trip to town, a journey of any kind from a casual ramble to a planned excursion. Don't try at this stage to make a record of where you're going, or what you may be watching. Look instead for single shots, or short sequences, and use them as assignments on which to practise your camera technique. When you can spot a promising link, or contrast, between one subject and another, and you can react smoothly and effectively to bring them together into a single shot, then you can think about moving on to a more planned and ambitious use of your video equipment. But first, it's necessary to learn something of the language . . .

CHAPTER ONE

THE GRAMMAR OF FILM-MAKING

Once the operation of the camcorder has become a simple, semi-automatic process, then it's time to start paying more attention to what to shoot, and why, and in what order. In other words, we need to pay attention to the grammar of film-making, and how it's used to tell a story, put over an argument, create an impression, or simply entertain your audience. And we need to begin by considering the individual shots which make up any production, from the simplest home video to a feature film or a television documentary.

Because it's possible to describe shots by a series of universally recognised names, it's equally possible to script a shoot by specifying a series of shots which can be detailed and described with the minimum of confusion. Once again, it's easier to understand what's involved by applying it to a genuine subject, so let's begin by finding a familiar subject which is easy to describe, easy to shoot and not likely to move off in the middle of the exercise. Something like, for example, three people sitting on a park bench. If they know you, and don't mind being part of your training, so much the better — otherwise, try and find people who, for whatever reason, are engrossed in what they're doing. They're less likely to move without warning, or to be irritated by your watching them through the camera lens.

FRAMING YOUR SHOT

All that remains is to switch on the camcorder, zoom in to hold the group in close-up, and adjust the focus. Depending on the distance between you and the subjects, and on the power of the lens fitted to

Figure 7. Three shots of the same group of people: a LONG SHOT (top), MEDIUM SHOT (centre) and a CLOSE-UP (bottom). The difference between these shots will depend on the distance between you and your subject and the power of your lens.

your camcorder, you might see the faces of all three people in the viewfinder — or just one. Let's assume, in this case , that you frame the picture on the face of the centre person of the three. This is a CLOSE-UP. If you then press on the zoom control to pull right back to the opposite end of the zoom, you will have the three people and the seat in the centre of the picture, together with their surroundings and something of the foreground separating you from them. This has now become a LONG SHOT. If you then zoom back halfway to the CLOSE-UP position, you will be looking at a MEDIUM SHOT. Broadly speaking, these are the three basic types of shot from which sequences and programmes are constructed.

Of course, there has to be a great deal more to it than that. If you were shooting, or scripting, a genuine programme, then you need more detailed and more specific descriptions. So let's take a closer look — literally. Imagine that we want a closer view of an individual's face, to register a subtle facial reaction, or a change of emotion which might be missed if we watched from too far away. By moving the camera or using the zoom, or both, you close in until the frame is filled by the eyes, nose and mouth of the subject. This is what's usually known as a BIG CLOSE-UP. Move in closer still, to concentrate on just the eyes, or the mouth, of the subject, and you have an EXTREME CLOSE-UP. All these terms are relative, and they're usually referred to by their initials in a script or shot-list: LS, MS, CU, BCU and ECU for these examples.

The same graduation between one type of shot and another happens as you zoom out, or move the camera back away from the subject. Move back out far enough from the group to see all three figures, and you have what might be described as a MEDIUM CLOSE-UP — halfway between our CLOSE-UP and our MEDIUM SHOT. Move back further still, and you have the MEDIUM SHOT we looked at earlier. Futher back again, and we're looking at a MEDIUM LONG SHOT and finally, with the subject at the maximum distance away, we're back at our LONG SHOT. Or, in certain circumstances, it's called a WIDE SHOT; there's no hard and fast rule about which term you use.

But which is the right term to use? It really depends on the context, and how it appears in the frame. If, for example, your close-up subject is seen further down a path or a road from the camera position, so that when you pull back to the opposite end of the zoom, you're more conscious of the increasing distance between camera and subject, then it's clearly a LONG SHOT. If, on the other hand, you pull out and the additional area now covered in the frame is made up of a wider and less specific foreground, like open grassland, then a WIDE SHOT may well be the more appropriate description. The point to remember is that there are no hard and fast rules — the description is more a matter of common sense than anything else.

Figure 8. Another LONG SHOT (above) and an EXTREME CLOSE-UP (left) of part of the same picture — in this case, the rear hub-cap of the car.

In fact, you'll see that these terms are anything but rigid. They have to be capable of being used to suit any kind of subject and any kind of variation between an EXTREME CLOSE-UP and EXTREME LONG SHOT of that subject. In some cases, you may use a different set of definitions to make the distinction clear.

Before we look at the problems of choosing and framing individual shots to make the best of a subject, there's another kind of shot description which is worth knowing about. It's used in interviews, in drama, or in any other situation where people are talking to one another.

It works like this. Let's imagine now that our three people are in conversation. One of them is an interviewer, and the other two are answering his questions. You may want to introduce the group by a shot which shows the trio filling the frame. This is often described as a THREE-SHOT. You may want to concentrate on the interviewer, in which case you follow it with a CLOSE-UP (INTERVIEWER). Then you may want to show the reaction of both the interviewees to one of his questions but, for variety, you don't want to see the whole group again. So this time you frame the shot so that you can only see the two people being interviewed, in which case — logically enough — it's a TWO-SHOT. If you go back to the group, it's a THREE-SHOT again, and then if you concentrate on one person answering a single question then it's another CLOSE-UP, and so on.

It's important to remember that these shot descriptions are just that: shorthand classifications to indicate a type of shot, rather than a hard and fast definition of how a shot should be set up and framed. Because, in the end, how you compose a shot depends on you: the camera operator. It can be a matter of inspiration but, on the other hand, there are guidelines which can be learned to help you get it right. Keep to these, and in time framing will become second nature to you. But always, above all, keep a weather eye open for the unusual, the interesting, or the unexpected. Remember that an unusual view of a familiar sight is worth taking a little extra trouble over.

So let's start setting up some shots. To begin with, look for a static subject — coping with moving ones is a special technique we'll come to later. This time we're not looking for a single subject which we'll

36

treat in different ways between a long shot and a close-up, as we did before. Instead, we should be looking for different types of subject, so that we can explore the different types of framing which will draw attention to different facets of each subject.

COMPOSING YOUR SHOT

Let's take a typical holiday situation — a day at the seaside, with crowds on the promenade, on the beach, in the water and in and out of the shops and cafés along the seafront. It's a familiar situation, but also one with plenty in it for the camera: people relaxing, people swimming, people paddling, people concentrating on anything from eating an ice cream to the prices in a shop window display. All offer excellent potential — especially children, who are more involved in what they're doing than adults, and who (provided they're not aware of the camera) are generally less self-conscious about their self-absorption. Don't worry at this stage about trying to tell an involved story or put over a complex picture of all that meets your eye, and your camera lens. Keep it simple: go instead for a series of brief glimpses of the interesting, the varied and the unexpected.

The first thing to remember is that, unlike the specialist stills photographer, who can trim and crop his prints to make the very best of a particular subject, you're always stuck with the proportions of the television screen — four units wide and three units deep. Within those confines, you have to make each picture you shoot look attractive and well composed. With faces, the rules are fairly easy to summarise: if you're framing the whole face, then give it sufficient room. Don't let the top of the head touch the top of your frame, or let the chin of your subject touch the bottom of your frame, or your picture will look crowded and badly composed. If you want to go for a bigger close-up view, then close in so that the top of the head is definitely out of frame, but there is still space below the subject's chin. Closer still, and both hairline and chin are well beyond the top and bottom of the frame.

Figure 9. Different ways of framing the face: always remember to avoid letting the top of the head just touch the top of the frame, or the chin just touch the bottom of the frame — either will make the picture look cramped.

If your subject is looking more or less straight at the camera, then they can be framed close to the centre of your picture area. If, on the other hand, your subject is definitely looking at something, or talking to someone who is out of frame to the right of your picture area, then you need to frame them towards the left of the picture. It's a question of leaving sufficient room on the side to which they're looking or speaking, to avoid the picture appearing cramped or crowded. Having said that, though, there are times when all these rules might need to be broken — for example, you may have two or three people in shot, all of whom are looking in that same direction, when your margin on the right-hand side of the frame will be much smaller. The important thing in all these areas is to know what the rules are and to know why you're breaking them, if that seems the way to produce the shot you want.

In terms of longer or wider shots, the rules are rather different. Because the television screen is so much smaller than the cinema screen, fine detail tends to be lost. This means that to tell a story in television terms, each shot has a tighter and more specific job to do — to cover a detail in a picture, or a person's reaction, you need a close-up. To cover the context, the background or the other elements in the story, you need a medium shot or a long/wide shot, and to keep the audience informed and move the story along, you need to change from one type of shot to another in quick succession. As an example, try watching a television drama or documentary and note how the camera changes from long or wide shots to medium shots and close-ups in covering the subject.

Back now to our seaside subject. We want a shot to set the scene with — for example, an open stretch of beach, with some people paddling along the shoreline. If can often be helpful to split the frame into thirds, horizontally and vertically, and set out to place the areas of most interest in your picture along these dividing lines, or at the intersections between the horizontal and vertical divisions, for an attractive composition. In this case, we might decide to set the horizon along the horizontal line two-thirds of the way up our frame. We might also decide to set the distant figures of the picture, if they're the chief focus of interest in the shot, at the point where the lower horizontal dividing line intersects with one of the vertical dividing lines. But which one should we choose?

If the shot is simple, the direction in which your paddlers are walking could decide which of those imaginary vertical lines you use to place them in the frame. If they're walking from left to right, then placing them one-third of the way into the picture from the left-hand side would leave them plenty of walking room — if they are walking from right to left, then move them over to the right-hand third of the frame. Either way, you should end up with a well-composed picture.

Figure 10. *Always bear in mind the proportions of your picture — four units broad and three deep. Think of the picture area as divided into thirds, and try to frame your subject so that the main areas of interest tend to fall close to the dividing lines between these horizontal and vertical thirds.*

Figure 11. *A well-composed picture, with the main point of interest — the engine driver — framed according to the thirds rule. Notice also that there is more space in the frame in the direction to which he's looking — the so-called 'looking room'.*

Before we leave the subject of long shots, it's important to remember the third dimension. Distant subjects are small and far away on the television screen, so that movement and depth are greatly diminished. This means that long shots can have a very two-dimensional feel about them, which gives them a remoteness you may not want in your sequence. Although there are times when you may want to stress that feeling of distance and separation for very good and positive reasons, in most cases this will be an effect you want to avoid — so always look for a detail in the foreground which can add depth to the picture, and help tie the more distant view to the immediate surroundings from which you're shooting.

LINKING PARTS OF A SCENE

There are several ways of doing this, each with advantages and drawbacks which have to be taken into account. The simplest is to frame your shot so that something which is closer to the camera (but still far enough away to be in focus at the same time as the most distant part of your shot) can help to fill the foreground. This can also add a link with your previous shot in a sequence, to place the current shot in its correct context. If, for example, your previous shot was a close-up of a candy-floss stall on the promenade, then including part of the promen-ade railings or the staircase down to the beach, on one side of your frame, will provide that link and add the depth you want to the shot. In other cases, though, it may be a nearer group of people sleeping in their deckchairs — less a visual link to another shot than a way of balancing the current picture to better effect.

Of course there are ways in which you can link the foreground and the background more directly within the same shot. For example, you can do what we practised earlier on — begin with the shot of the candy-floss stall on the promenade, and pan slowly round to pick up the wide stretch of beach with the group of people paddling at the water's edge. Or you can start off with the long shot of the paddlers in the distance and zoom slowly in until they fill as much of the frame as possible. Remember what we said earlier about slowness and steadiness, and keep the opening and closing frames for a second each.

There's an even more ambitious combination of pan and zoom it might be worthwhile to try. Start this time from the candy-floss stall on the promenade,

41

and pan round till the paddlers come into your frame. Continue the pan and start zooming towards the figures, so that ideally you end the pan and the zoom at the same time with your distant figures filling the frame. It's a complex process to get right, so try several takes to see where and when to start and finish the two movements relative to one another. If you can combine the two movements smoothly and attractively, it can make for a genuinely beautiful and powerful shot, where the camera movements are used to satisfying effect.

Of course, not all visual links have to be so ambitious. There is another way in which you can use the zoom in linking two different parts of a scene. Looking at a distant subject through the close-up end of the zoom has two very obvious effects. First, that part of the scene is foreshortened, so that objects which may be a fair distance apart, but which are even further from the camera, look as if they're very close together.

The other effect, which makes a different kind of transition shot possible, is that the depth of field of the lens (the range of distances over which objects are all in focus for a given setting) is shorter at a close-up setting of the zoom than it would be for a wide shot. So objects which may appear close together in this kind of shot may — if they're far enough apart in reality — give the game away by one object appearing in focus, and the other one being sufficiently out of focus to be a vague and mysterious image.

All the camera operator has to do to make the transition between one image and the other is to hold the camera very still and turn the focus ring slowly. One object will then slowly melt out of focus while the other one sharpens and becomes clear. It's a neat technique, but you can only use it when the two subjects between them fill the frame, and when the difference in distance is enough to make the change-focus effect work.

Sometimes you can actually see one object through the other — a child playing seen through a set of playground railings, for example — and this makes the change-focus a specially attractive shot. But, as always with tricky shots like this, remember two things above all. Hold the camera as steadily as you can, and try the shot several times until you're pleased with the effect before you actually record it. That's another reason for picking reasonably static subjects at this stage of your experience with the camcorder.

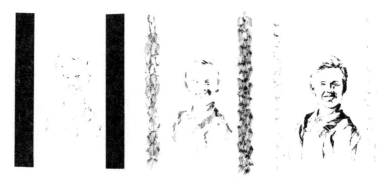

Figure 12. A change-focus shot as a way of linking subject and surroundings. The playground railings are seen in sharp focus with the little boy in the background as a faint blur (left), then, as you adjust the focus, the bars of the railings move out of focus as the boy becomes more distinct (centre), until finally the railings become a faint blur leaving the boy in sharp focus (right).

VARYING THE PERSPECTIVE

There are other ideas you can use to make your shots more varied. Since we see the world from our own eye level, it seems logical to shoot from roughly that level for most of the time. But now and again you can create a different effect by shooting a subject from very low down. This can magnify the size of a person or an object, and make them look much more dominant and imposing. Or you can position yourself and the camera so you're looking down at the subject instead, which can add a sense of detachment and secrecy — almost as if the camera is eavesdropping on what is happening below.

Another convention is that the horizon should always be horizontal, and lines which would be vertical in the real world should always be vertical in the picture. Tilting the camera so that the horizon slants from one corner of the picture to the other can be very powerful in conveying unreality or uncertainty — try it out for yourself on a familiar object, like the people walking along the promenade, and see what feelings it creates in the finished shot. But if you use this effect in a programme, always do it for a genuine reason, or the audience may find it irritating or confusing.

Above all, always be on the lookout for the unexpected. A shot of a Punch-and-Judy show is a familiar and attractive detail of a day at the seaside — but a shot of the Punch-and-Judy man sitting beside the booth and getting his puppets ready before the performance would provide a more unusual perspective. Shots of children playing beach cricket, or queuing for an ice cream, or staring in toyshop windows all qualify as useful subjects — but look for the odd face which may be sleepy, or unhappy, or bored, to provide balance and variety. Above all, try and choose your shots so that the audience will be in no doubt about the main point of interest in each case. Don't include a sleeping child and a parent reading a newspaper unless you're establishing a definite link — either concentrate on one or the other, or make the link clear by how you frame both subjects in the shot. If your audience isn't able to follow your intentions by spotting the main focal point of the shot, then you haven't framed the shot properly.

There are exceptions to this rule, however. Sometimes you come across a subject which has an appeal of its own, over the whole of the frame rather than a particular focal point. A city crowd rushing from station to office may present itself through your viewfinder as a sea of faces, all walking towards you, and filling the whole of the frame. An endless succession of feet on a staircase, or even a line of repeated objects — all these shots have a visual

44

rhythm which gives them an individual appeal, and it's worth being on the lookout for this kind of effect, wherever — and whatever — you're shooting. Even in a vintage car rally, a long line of parked cars stretching right into the distance has this magical quality of visual rhythm which makes it worth capturing on tape.

Figure 13. Two examples of visual rhythm in the same subject — repeated heads and figures seen by shooting a line of people from one end, and the repetition of the lines of bandsmen moving through the frame make for a very effective shot.

In the end, it's impossible to give a set of hard and fast rules to cover every subject, and every situation. Most of all, learning to set up, frame, and capture shots is a matter of practice, so that you know what you're looking for, and you can recognise a good subject when it stares you in the viewfinder. The more you can develop a good picture sense, and the more developed your sense of composition, the more quickly you can react to your subjects, and the more enjoyment you'll derive from your video-making.

So keep on shooting and analysing your shots — while you're rehearsing them, while you're shooting them, and while you're watching them being played back on the screen. Was your framing tight enough, without being too tight? Was the prime interest in your picture clearly and properly displayed? Did the

45

shot do what you wanted it to do? Did you shoot a close-up when you should have used a medium shot to do the subject justice? The happier you feel with your shots, as shots, rather than as part of a planned and structured programme, the sooner you'll be able to move on to the next stage of video production: taking all the shots we've been looking at and linking them into a properly planned and edited sequence.

CHAPTER TWO

TELLING THE STORY

The first chapter set out to look at the different types of shot which can be used to build up a sequence — how to recognise them, how to frame them and how to shoot them. Now we're going to look at how to plan them — how long they should last, when they should stop, and how to cut or move from one to the next so that the final sequence is varied, interesting and full of pace — entertaining your audience — rather than boring or predictable.

First of all though, let's be aware of what *not* to do. If you look at most unskilled amateur videos, they tend to suffer from one common fault. Whatever the quality of the equipment, whatever the interest of the subject, the person operating the camera seems to be unaware of how to stop recording. One shot leads straight into another; in fact, the programme becomes a single shot for minutes on end, with the camera panning right and left and zooming in and out, and even just wobbling uncertainly from one part of the scene to another.

Sometimes you find yourself watching one subject, then, for no clearly apparent reason, the camera's attention wanders to a different subject, then back to the first one. Sometimes in the middle of a move from one subject to another, the camera operator will have second thoughts, and swing back to the first subject again. The camera movements resemble someone using a hose to water a lawn, wash a car, or put out a small fire. They wander restlessly backwards and forwards, until the whole area has been throughly soaked.

No wonder this approach to shooting is often called 'hosepipe direction', and it's the clearest giveaway of all that the person behind the camera has no clear idea of what he or she is doing. They're simply reacting to the subject, rather than imposing their own plans, ideas, and objectives on the material they are trying to record. And the result is that the recording is tiring, distracting, and boring to watch — quite literally, a waste of time and tape.

THE DISCIPLINE OF SHOOTING

So one of the most important controls on any camcorder is the 'stop' or 'pause' button — the one which ends the shot before it overstays its welcome on the screen, or before the next camera movement becomes irritating, misplaced or confusing. It's difficult to specify the length of time a particular shot should last, since so much depends on the visual interest of whatever it is you may be watching. But as a rough guide, a wide shot with a fair degree of activity could last up to ten seconds if there is a lot of information for the audience to register. If, on the other hand, the movement is limited, and the picture is a fairly simple one to establish, then five seconds would be more appropriate.

Some shots need to be shorter. A quickly-paced sequence telling a story in short, simple close-ups could have each shot on the screen for as little as a couple of seconds apiece. Others might need to be longer: a shot of an airliner about to touch down on an airport runway cries out to be followed at least until the wheels touch the ground, and for a second or two beyond, or the cut away to the next subject will seem badly timed. But if the action is unnecessarily prolonged, your audience will lose interest, and if something is bound to take time, then you need to consider the possibility of cutaways.

To take our previous example, if you have a shot of the airliner coming in over the boundary fence of the airfield, you don't need to follow it all the way down to the ground in a single shot which may last for thirty or forty seconds. Better to stay with the approaching plane for ten seconds at the most, then switch to shoot something else appropriate to the location — faces of the visitors in the terminal viewing gallery for example — before cutting back for a ten-second shot of the touchdown proper. That way, it's easy to maintain the pace without missing any of the vital action.

Until you've had sufficient practice, however, it makes a lot of sense to consider these points in advance, and work out a basic shooting plan. It doesn't have to be a complete script, or even a section of script. It might only cover two or three shots at a time, and it might not even have to be written down on paper. The essential thing is to *think* about what you're going to shoot, and the subjects you will be looking out for. With a plan, however sketchy, you have a blueprint to work to. Without a plan, there's the danger you may let a shot go on too long, or — worse still — change your mind in mid-shot and drift off into an unplanned and uncontrolled camera movement which spoils the rhythm and the pace of the sequence you're building up.

So the next step in producing a professional home video is to learn the value of discipline. This means deciding very firmly what each shot is *for*, what you should be looking at, and why, what subjects you are trying to link together, what effects you are trying to create, how a particular shot relates to the previous shot, and how it will relate to its successors. When you have thought about all these matters, and decided exactly what you want the shot to achieve, then you will have fixed what kind of shot it should be. You'll have fixed where it should start, where it should finish, and more or less how long it should last. All you have to do is rehearse the shot, modify it wherever you feel it might be improved, and then record it.

The discipline comes in sticking precisely to the plan you have worked out in your head and rehearsed beforehand. Don't change your mind in mid-shot. If you have a sudden flash of inspiration, or if some change in the subject opens up another, better possibility, finish your shot first. Only then decide whether or not it's worth replacing it with a different version, or whether your first idea was better after all. It may well be that you can have the best of both worlds, and think of another view of the subject which follows logically after the shot you have just recorded. We'll look at how to build up a sequence of shots later. In the meantime there's the second aspect of self-discipline to consider, and the hardware which will help you to achieve it.

It's all to do with keeping a steady picture. Even if careful planning and a refusal to be diverted from the plan does manage to avoid the worst outbreaks of the hosepipe effect, it's still essential to hold the camera as steadily as possible while you're recording. This too requires practice. Even for a skilled and experienced cameraman, keeping the camera still during a long and careful zoom is a very difficult proposition.

It's even worse if you need to keep looking at something at the close-up end of the zoom for a long time, since every movement of the camera will seem magnified when you watch the shot on play-back afterwards. So it's essential to think in terms of a tripod to support the camera for you, and to help you with the more difficult transition shots. In fact it's probably fair to say that next to your camcorder, the tripod is the most important item of video equipment.

In a way, it may seem odd to consider fastening your light and compact camcorder to a heavy and un-wieldy tripod, when the manufacturers have done all they can to make the unit easy to carry and small enough to pack away when you're on the move. But the same has been true of stills cameras for a long time, yet serious stills photographers know only too well how essential a tripod can be for certain types of photography. It isn't really a question of needing a tripod — as used to be the case — to reduce the sheer fatigue of supporting a heavy and awkwardly-balanced piece of equipment through a day's shooting. Much more important is the steadying effect of a good tripod, and the kind of polished, professional shooting it makes possible, even with the lightest and most compact camcorders of all. But it has to be the *right* kind of tripod.

CHOOSING AND USING A TRIPOD

If you are using a tripod with an ordinary stills camera, then it has a fairly simple job to do — to hold your camera steady for the duration of the exposure, which even in very low light isn't likely to be more than a minute at the most. This type of tripod may be suitable for use with a video camera too, if your main purpose is to find a camera platform for static shots, or the kind of absolutely standard zooms in and out, where the camera doesn't move at all — in these cases the lens system, and the subject, do all the moving for you.

But this is only part of what a tripod should be capable of, in making a movie programme. Take a close look at any feature film or television documentary, and you'll find the camera is on the move for a great deal of the time. Apart from panning and tilting shots, there are combinations of pans and tilts and zooms for covering complex transitions from one subject to another, which would need a great deal of experience (and quite a few attempts) to get right with a shoulder-supported camera.

So can a tripod help? Yes, if it's the right type of tripod, or if you know what its limitations are. All camera tripods will have a mounting platform for the camera, which can be panned and tilted so that you can aim the camera at the subject, wherever it is. There will also be a pair of locking wheels or butterfly nuts which allow you to fix the camera at the desired angle. This is fine for static shots, but the locks need to be loosened for anything which requires the camera itself to move. And this is where the problems start. When you start to pan, for example, you have to overcome any friction within the tripod before the camera platform begins to pivot. But because static friction is greater than rolling friction, once you've overcome that resistance, you'll suddenly need less force to keep the camera panning.

What this means in practice is that the pan often starts with a perceptible jerk, as the platform suddenly starts to move. The pan may then be steady enough, but as you slow down at the end of it the frictional resistance of the tripod head will suddenly re-assert itself, and the pan will stop with another perceptible snatch. To solve this problem, professional tripods often have heavy, fluid-mounted heads which smooth out these start/stop transitions as far as possible, and make the movement as smooth as possible. But they're heavy, cumbersome and expensive, so the chances are you'll have to manage with a tripod less well suited to the job in hand.

What's the answer? Once again, it's all down to practice. The more you can accustom yourself to the amount of effort needed to start and stop a pan or a tilt smoothly, and the right amount of friction you need to set with the locking adjustments on the tripod head to make this possible, the better your shots will be. But make sure the tripod itself is heavy enough for the job. When you *want* a static camera position, is the tripod strong enough to support the camera securely? Or does it shudder under every gust of wind, so that close-ups become difficult to do, even with the tripod to help you?

Tripods do need to be used carefully. If you plan to record a shot which involves panning and tilting, then you will have to loosen both adjustments to make it possible to move the head smoothly. But when your shot is finished, make sure you lock the camera platform securely. Otherwise, as soon as you let go of the tripod handle, the weight of the camera will tilt it forwards or backwards quite sharply, depending on the positioning of the tripod mounting and the camera's own centre of gravity. Either way, you could easily damage the camera — and if it tilts backwards, the lens could point directly at the sun, causing internal damage if it's fitted with tubes.

There are two other problems worth bearing in mind when you're using a tripod. One is that you may well find, when you're panning to follow a moving object, that the object may also move up or down when you're not expecting it to, so you could find it vanishing through the top or bottom of your frame. And the other problem is that tripods themselves could have been designed just for people to trip over their outstretched legs. Watch that no-one ruins your shot by catching a tripod leg at the wrong moment — at the very least you'll have a spoiled shot but, at the worst, you could damage the camera or cause an injury to someone. And that includes you. When you're concentrating hard on what you're seeing through the viewfinder in a difficult pan, it's all too easy to trip over your own tripod legs.

In buying a tripod, it's wise to look for the very best you can afford. One day, you may want to exchange your camera for a more professional or versatile one, but a good tripod will always stand you in good stead. And the more features it carries, the more it will improve your shooting, whatever the quality of the camera you may be using, either now, or in the future.

What kind of features should the ideal tripod have? A fluid-mounted head, if you can afford one, since this will make the most difference to the smoothness and professionalism of your shooting. Strong construction — camcorders are now considerably lighter than cine cameras, but you want a tripod which is not only going to support your camera without the threat of failure, but is going to provide a *steady* mounting for your moving shots. A good range of adjustments on the tripod legs is a worthwhile feature — extendible legs allow you to shoot from a viewpoint higher than eye level, if you can find a suitable box to stand on to reach the camera controls. And legs which can be splayed to an almost horizontal position give you the option of the occasional low-level shot when holding the camera steady without the tripod might be difficult, or even impossible.

Another useful feature is a spirit level on the tripod mounting. If you're setting up for a pan with the background in shot, then you want the camera to be level all the way round the pan. One way of doing this is to set the tripod up, and then pan the camera round while checking that the horizon remains level all the way. But this can be a cumbersome and time-consuming business: it's far easier to check with a built-in spirit level that everything is level before you start.

Some tripods can even be fitted with a set of wheels. This gives you the option of yet another shot — the tracking shot — where the camera and tripod move bodily while shooting, either to follow a moving subject backwards, forwards or sideways, or to bring a different perspective to a scene by moving the camcorder through it.

Successful tracking shots depend on a number of factors — among them the smoothness of the surface over which the tripod wheels will be tracking — but once again, practice makes perfect. The start of the shot, when the camera moves from the static position to the start of its tracking movement, and the end, where it comes to a stop again, are the most difficult parts to get right. But if these difficulties can be overcome, there are some striking effects which a good tracking shot can achieve, and which make it worth bearing in mind as a creative device.

Are there any alternatives to a tripod, if a good one is too expensive, or if you don't have one with you? The most distracting camera movement is usually the up-and-down one. If you can keep the camera steady in the horizontal plane, then achieving steady shots, and steady pans, is much easier. So a simple camera support, leaving you to make these movements by hand, can be a worthwhile alternative to completely hand-held operation. You can opt for the kind of monopod — a single, telescopic leg with a camera mounting at the top — which stills cameramen use, as a viable alternative to the tripod in some

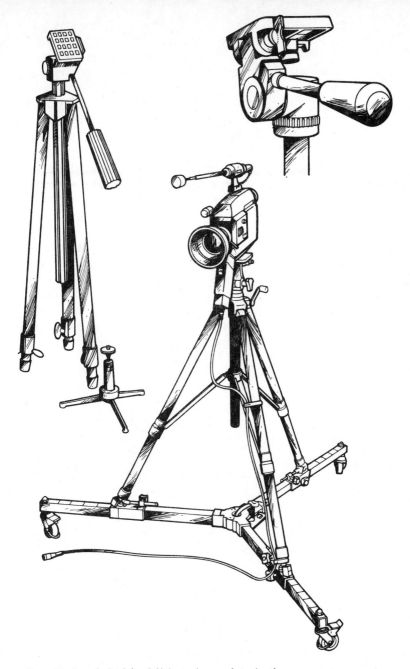

Figure 14. A good tripod (top left) is sturdy enough to give the camera proper support and allow you to carry out pans and zooms. Below it is a mini tripod (or set of 'baby legs') useful for allowing really low camera viewpoints. The adjustment of the friction head (top right) is crucial for smooth camera movements. Some tripods can be fitted with wheels (bottom picture) to allow tracking shots on specially smooth surfaces.

cases. Pans will be easier than they will be without any extra support, and there's none of the inherent frictional problems there would be with the cheaper and simpler tripod heads. It's also easier to follow a moving subject and cater for any unexpected dips or swoops by tilting the leg of the monopod backwards or forwards enough to keep the subject in the frame. The monopod is also lighter than any worthwhile tripod, and worth bearing in mind whenever the subject matter requires that portability and speed of movement from place to place are important considerations.

If even a monopod is out of the question on a particular shoot, then keep an eye open for any source of support at all. You can steady a shot by finding a convenient wall to lean on — either a horizontal surface to support your arms, and the camera, or a vertical wall against which you can lean bodily while concentrating on steadying the camera.

Figure 15. Sometimes you may find a tripod is too cumbersome. Other options (left to right) include leaning against a wall to steady the camera, using a monopod, or strong elastic to a foot stirrup or a belt to reduce any tendency towards camera shake.

56

And there's even a dodge for tracking shots without tripods. If you can find any kind of transport, from a supermarket trolley to a wheelchair, get someone to push you through the tracking movement, while you sit in the chair and cradle the camera as steadily as you can. With a little bit of practice on your part, and that of the person pushing you, the results can be surprisingly effective.

PLANNING A SEQUENCE

Once you've practised these different types of shot, with whatever equipment you're able to lay your hands on, you can now turn to look at how shots can be linked together to make a sequence on a particular subject. At this stage, we will assume that you are effectively editing in the machine which you're using to record. In other words, the order in which you shoot the shots will be the order in which they will appear in the finished sequence. This means thinking very carefully about each shot in turn, but there's no reason why the finished sequence need not be as polished and professional as it would be if you were able to edit and reshuffle and select from the material afterwards — as a professional production team would be able to do.

In some cases, this need to assemble your production in real time poses less of a problem. In covering an event, for example, your approach is basically that of a news cameraman, in that you are likely to be responding to events as they happen, and telling a story in more or less the sequence in which your shots will be recorded. But this in turn imposes some restrictions on how you work. You may be able to do some planning in advance but, in most respects, you will have to depend on thinking quickly at the time, to make sure that what you're shooting will build up to a logical and entertaining view of the day's happenings. Don't, therefore, set out to be too ambitious at this stage. If you are planning to cover a horse-racing meeting, a football match or a motor race, it's usually pointless to try to cover the action in the same way as a live television broadcast would do.

There are two reasons for this: live television would be able to deploy people and resources on a totally different scale, to ensure that the whole of the action could be captured. Were they restricted to a single camera crew, even with fully professional equipment, the view of the proceedings they'd be able to cover would be as limited as yours — apart from better arrangements they might be able to make in terms of access, or viewpoints, for example. Secondly, even if you *were* able to cover all the action of the afternoon, would your audience really want to watch it? Horse races and motor races are, generally speaking, catering for an audience of knowledgeable and dedicated enthusiasts for those particular sports. Leaving aside the people who watch horse races because of a betting interest, even the wider audience for these events won't be worried about the length of the programme, or the repetition as one race, or one stage of the race, succeeds another. Your audience may well lose interest long before, however professionally you cover the subject.

So let's accept our limitations, and the interests of our audience. They may not have enough dedicated enthusiasm, or background knowledge, to want to watch a long programme about horse racing, or motor racing, but, for that very reason, they might well find it interesting to catch a glimpse of what goes on as the meeting runs its course. The atmosphere, the details and the appeal of the unexpected — objectives which can be covered with a camcorder and a good deal of inspiration and planning — are what will interest them, and help to make for a fresh and original programme.

This means you need to do some homework first. In fact, it's a good idea to begin with what professionals call a 'recce' (short for reconnaissance). All it means is visiting a race meeting, preferably on the location where you plan to shoot, but without a camera. In the case of a three-day horse-racing event, you can go on the day before you plan to shoot. In the case of a motor-race meeting, do your recce on one of the practice days, when there will be everything there except the crowds, so you'll be able to enjoy a good clear view of proceedings.

It's essential to remember one point before you even start. This is just a preliminary exercise intended to build up some simple but entertaining sequences. But it's also building up your familiarity, both with the equipment and, more importantly still, with the need to think like a film-maker. So it is worth approaching it properly, with an eye to the unusual, the interesting and the entertaining, as if you had a genuine audience in mind — even if, at this stage, your efforts are going to be seen, and criticised, and improved upon, by yourself alone.

Right, we'll assume you've arrived at the racetrack, and you're having your first look around. Try, first of all, to find a viewpoint which will let you capture an interesting wide shot of the whole location. This will set the scene, and allow you to follow it with a varied selection of closer shots, and it will also allow you a view of the proceedings which might give you some pointers as to where those close-up subjects might be found.

There are three particular questions to ask yourself at this stage. Is there enough in the foreground to give depth to the scene, and help provide a point of interest on which you, and the audience, can focus? Secondly, can you see other worthwhile subjects from your chosen camera position — can you zoom in for glimpses of the action, without having to move and set up again somewhere else — and capture the start, the finish line, the faces in the crowd? Finally, will you be able to see over the heads of the crowd on the day itself, and move when and where you want to? It might be worth considering a viewpoint further back from the action — if a little extra height will help to solve these problems — and recces help you to make decisions like these well in time for the event itself.

Next, you need to look around for promising close-up subjects. Your objective should be the kind of

Figure 16. Too much sky in the picture, especially on a dull day, can turn objects into silhouettes (top). One way out is to shoot down from an elevated viewpoint to reduce the amount of sky in the picture (below).

detail which can illuminate a totally unexpected facet of an otherwise familiar occasion. It might be a corner of the paddock, before a motor-race meeting, where you can shoot the racing cars being unloaded from their trailers and transporters, or mechanics making careful adjustments, or the drivers trying to relax over a drink or magazine before it's time to get ready for the race. It might be the members of one of the pit crews assembling the signal boards, to wave them in the faces of their drivers as they roar down the pit straight and give them much-needed information on their times, their positions, and their performance against the opposition. It might be something very fleeting, which you may all too easily miss, the pressing of a stop watch and the look of delight on the timekeeper's face at a really outstanding lap time. Candid glimpses of actions like these are food and drink to the keen film-maker, and can help provide a totally individual and absorbing view of the most hackneyed event.

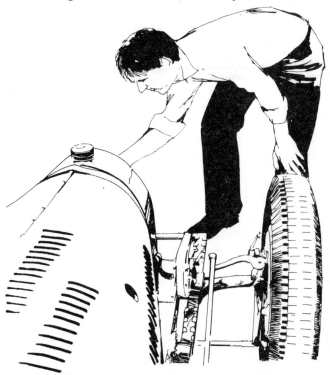

Figure 17. *Always be on the lookout for the unexpected — like the careful polishing of a contender at a vintage-car race meeting.*

Don't underestimate the power of research to help you find what you want. In this case, all it means is speaking to someone who's a regular visitor to race meetings, preferably at the location we're looking at. They may well know where the jockeys queue for the weighing-in, where you can stand for a good view of the winning owners and their horses after the race, or whether there's a useful shot of picnic parties to be recorded during gaps in the action. Always remember, though, to check for access on the day itself. Having to pay to move to different stands and enclosures can take time, and add to the cost of covering the event.

There are certain principles which apply to whatever subject you choose for your first sequence. Both horse racing and motor racing satisfy two requirements as programme subjects. They're full of colour, and they're full of movement. Generally speaking, television — or video — doesn't treat static subjects well at all. The medium lacks the quality, in terms of sharpness and clarity, which top-class photographs and slides can deliver. So where a subject is static by its nature, then it often calls for a top-quality presenter to lend it the interest and movement it would otherwise lack.

As a general rule, though, be on the lookout for change, as well as movement. During a vintage car rally, try to concentrate on a moment when something definite is going on. Either the cars are arriving and being marshalled into orderly lines in the car park, or the judges are walking around checking which ones are worthy of prizes — or the prizes themselves are actually being handed over to the winners. It isn't a bad idea to note whether all the other people on the scene are watching you, or whether they're looking at whatever it is you're shooting. If they're looking at you, then it's fairly certain that your subject isn't interesting enough on its own. Look for something which is successful in distracting everyone's attention from you and your camcorder. At the very least, it will mean less of the waving hands and stares into the camera which can ruin the best-planned shots at the worst possible moment.

Having found a good subject, where there's plenty of action and interest, try to plan how you'll capture it with the camera. It's easier to cope with action which is continuing, or which is predictable, than something which happens quickly and with little warning. For example, a race where cars are going round and round a track gives you time to shoot your sequence in whatever order you like — the timed departure, or arrival, of a train gives you something to work towards in building up your sequence. A sudden passing car, or a low-flying aeroplane, may be a dramatic event, but you won't have the time or the warning to do it justice.

You can always include the odd static subject, provided it's kept brief, and provided it has a place in the sequence. For example, the notice board with the names of the runners — or a display of the race details to identify the event we're waiting for — acts as graphics in telling part of the story for you. Generally speaking, you need to keep these shots running for as long as it takes people to read the name, or the information, twice, very slowly. This is because the audience has to have time to react before they can start absorbing the information.

If your general shot and your close-ups have worked so far, you can now try to build up a second sequence of a particular activity which is going on. And this is where you need to bear two more factors in mind: continuity and cutaways.

CONTINUITY AND CUTAWAYS

Both these factors arise out of another of the basic laws of film-making — the need to compress time as far as possible to make an interesting sequence out of something which would otherwise seem boring and predictable. We've already explained how you would never set out to show a race meeting in its entirety; a series of brief, varied glimpses combining the action and the unexpected details will suit your own experience and the attention span of your audience much better. And the restriction applies when you need to capture a particular activity as part of the story you're setting out to tell in pictures — the more everyday it is, the more briefly you need to hint at what's going on.

Let's take one example. Imagine, for a moment, that your coverage of the race meeting involves following two of the racegoers on their way to the course. They walk down the road and catch a bus, which drops them near the course entrance. Then they walk to the gates, pay their entrance fee, and walk onto the course to find the best position they can, as close to the rails and to the winning post as possible. The whole journey might easily take twenty minutes and, if you shot it all from start to finish, you would use up a large part of your tape producing a serious contender for the most-boring-video-of-all-time trophy. We all know what standing at a bus stop waiting for an overdue bus feels like, and we don't need reminding.

Of course, if there was an important part of your story taking place on the journey, then your priorities would be different. But it's worth cultivating the habit of being as miserly with your tape as possible — only consider shooting a subject when it's interesting or attractive in its own right, or when you feel it's absolutely essential to the story you plan to tell. If we need to know how our racegoers got to the meeting, then try to compress it into a few brief shots. One as they close the gate behind them and walk to the bus stop; another as the bus pulls up and they climb aboard; one as they get off the bus and walk in the direction of the course entrance; and another as they edge up to their chosen vantage point on the rails.

Keep the shots brief enough, and the sequence might take no more than thirty seconds of screen time at the outside — but this is where cutaways and continuity come in. Often you want to cut a shot too short for the movement involved to come to a stop — people walking past the camera, for example. If you end the shot before they've passed out of frame, and you start another shot featuring the same people, then they will appear to have jumped instantaneously from one background to the next. It's called a 'jump cut' and it's to be avoided at all costs.

There are two ways of avoiding this, without having to run a shot longer than you want to. If you can find a shot of something which is relevant to the sequence you're building up, but which is not contained in the shot you're currently recording, then you can cut to that without having to wait for your people to walk completely out of frame. In this case, it might be a shot of the service timetable mounted on the bus-stop sign, or perhaps the approaching bus itself. When that shot has run as long as you want it to — say two to three seconds — you can cut back to the next shot of your group of people. The time interval provided by your cutaway shot will deliver the pause you need to be able to pose your next shot wherever you like.

What happens if you haven't got a suitable cutaway subject, or if you have reasons for following the action closely, but compressing the time taken as far as you can? That's where the question of continuity comes in. If you have a shot of your group of race-goers walking through the entrance turnstiles of the course, and then walking towards the camera, you can end that shot where you want to. All you have to do then is move your camera position so the next shot looks in the opposite direction, with the group walking away, as if they'd passed the camera. Because the backgrounds are so different, thanks to the camera looking in diametrically-opposed directions in the two shots, you can get away with moving your group much further on before shooting the second shot. But you *do* have to be careful about continuity. As far as possible, everything needs to be the same — the grouping of the people, their actions and their immediate surroundings. Don't have them ambling slowly in the first shot, and walking briskly or running in the second, or the cut won't work properly — and, although the backgrounds are different, their immediate surroundings must still correspond. If they're walking on grass in shot one, don't show them walking through a concrete car park in shot two. Preferably, the lighting conditions should match too — bright sunshine in the first shot and a cloudy patch in the second will make for a less subtle match, even if the shots were recorded within minutes of each other.

Remember, though, that techniques like these only work if they *look* credible. If you overdo the distance

Figure 18. Avoiding a jump cut without moving the camera — shoot the figure walking towards you (top picture), then start the next shot once they've passed you (lower picture).

that you move your camera between the walking-towards-you shot and the walking-away-from-you shot, then you may shorten the action of the walk so much that it fails to look convincing to your audience. That's the only test you have to pass with any techniques like this. If you can always be on the lookout for ways of shortening your shots and speeding up the action, then your programmes will be faster in pace, and any sections where you want to slow down the pace for other reasons will be much more effective as a result.

Keep on the lookout also, for anything which will make for an unusual or unexpected shot. If the weather has been wet, and there are puddles on the ground, then a different way of starting the shot where your party of racegoers is walking towards you is to shoot their reflections in the puddles, walking towards you apparently upside down. Give this image long enough to establish itself, say a couple of seconds as a guide, then pan upwards to show the people themselves in the usual way. If it's a bright, sunny day, then look for reflections in windows, car bodies and the like, to give an odd, slightly distorted view of reality. If you spot a subject with its own visual rhythm — like a sideways-on shot of the starting gate with the horses' heads lining up as they prepare for the race — then frame it to make the most of that rhythm, so it fills the screen, and include it at the right moment in your sequence. Another race-meeting possibility is a cutaway, while the race is in progress, looking along the rails rather than at the horses, and capturing the lines of faces showing a variety of emotions as the race progresses.

Figure 19. An ideal cutaway when covering a race meeting — the faces of the crowd watching the action, which gives you a shot which can be used almost anywhere in your sequence about the event.

VARYING YOUR SHOTS

Finally, as your shots build up on the tape, try to vary the type of shots you shoot in order, so that the framing and the viewpoint changes as much as possible. Don't cut from a wide shot of a scene to a close-up of part of that scene, from the same camera position, if you can help it. It's better by far to move the camera to get a different perspective, to go for a cutaway first, or to make a single shot from the two by zooming in from the wide shot to the close-up. If the framing of the opening wide shot doesn't place the close-up on which you want to end in the centre of the frame, then you'll have to pan across to end on the right part of the picture. So remember to check the focus at the close-up end of the shot first so that you know the shot will stay sharp right through the zoom, and try the combined zoom-and-pan movement a couple of times without recording, to make sure it is smooth and decisive when you *do* record. This means it's better to pick a subject which isn't going to move too quickly for you to cope with during all these steps — like the crowd facing you on the opposite side of the track, rather than the horses bearing down upon your camera position at full gallop!

For the time being, it might be better to think of starting each new subject with a wide shot to explain what it is we're looking at, then following it up with two, three or more closer shots — a combination of medium shots and close-ups, or of medium close-ups and big close-ups, to show the details of what's happening. This will depend to a certain extent on the scale of what we're seeing, and how far away it is from the camera position. For the presentation of the winner's trophy in a group of two or three people, with the horse and rider, then your establishing shot could well be a medium shot to begin with. This would be followed up by close-ups of the owner, the jockey, the horse's head and so on, before returning to the medium-shot frame for the handing over of the trophy. Back to close-ups for the reactions — the smile of the pleased owner, the applause from the onlookers — and perhaps a final medium shot as the horse is led away, before we look at the next subject.

This has been a very quick canter through several different areas of film-making. As a result, we've had to make a lot of assumptions and simplifications, with the overall objective of suggesting something to shoot as a way of becoming more familiar with using the camcorder equipment, thinking in sequences, and recognising and capturing promising material. At this stage, there's little point in going into more detail about programme planning and scripting, and the effects which particular shots and sequences can be used to create — all of this will be covered later. Far better, for the time being, to continue trying these approaches and techniques out on as many different subjects as possible. The varied experience you're building up will prove to be priceless later on, when you have more ambitious and more specific aims in mind. Review your work critically. Be on the lookout for mistakes and areas which could be improved, and in time you'll see your own work improving before your eyes — that's the best encouragement of all.

Figure 20. A simple sequence to cover the handover of the trophy: the winning horse being led into the enclosure (opposite, top), followed by shots of the owner and jockey (opposite, bottom) and the group with the trophy (above). These are the key shots, but the sequence should also include close-ups of faces, the horse's head, the trophy and any other interesting details.

CHAPTER THREE

FROM A CLEAN SHEET OF PAPER

In previous chapters, we began looking at some of the nuts and bolts of successful video programme-making — framing the shots, moving the camera, and thinking and shooting in sets of sequences. Now we need to look at how to produce a complete programme, which starts with the blueprint into which all these separate elements will have to fit. So we also need to understand how the different types of shots and camera movements are used, and the different effects they are intended to create. We need to understand how a programme idea is converted into a treatment, then a shooting script, and finally into a completed production. It really doesn't matter whether we're talking about a prime-time television documentary or a home video produced on a minute proportion of the budget, the equipment or the people. Both of them depend on the creative process, which gives them a great deal more in common than you might assume at first.

THE IDEA

The first step in making any kind of programme whatsoever is the original idea — the reason why the programme is being made. For a drama production, it could be a long-felt wish to translate the work of a well-established author into a series of television plays. Or it could be to make a programme on the latest production of your local amateur dramatic society. For documentary subjects, it could be a requirement to look at the implications of some new development in the power-politics of the Middle East — or it could be your niece's wedding. For a comedy, it could be a carefully-planned, cleverly-scripted and lavishly-casted sitcom — or it could be a tape of your last family holiday. For commercial purposes, it could be a television advertisement with a six-figure budget and a team of highly-paid specialists, or it could be a promotional tape for a local business, done as quickly and economically as possible.

All these programmes, and every other programme ever made, have to start off with an idea. Unfortunately, that's something no-one else can do for you — even suggestions will only work if they trigger off a development of that idea within your own mind. But it's possible to provide one or two guidelines, to help channel your thinking. For example, the professionals say that all television programmes should both entertain, and inform, in one way or another. Those aren't bad objectives for an amateur programme either — after all, if people aren't entertained, they won't want to keep on watching. Even if they are members of your family, it's much more satisfying to feel they're enjoying your tapes, rather than sitting through them out of duty and determination to endure to the end at all costs.

For a programme to be entertaining, it must also have other qualities. It needs to interest people, certainly, amuse them, very probably, surprise them and, occasionally, even stimulate them into taking action on something — even if it's to disagree violently with the approach the programme took because they think it too provoking!

For a programme to inform, it must tell (or show) the audience something they were not familiar with before they saw it. This could apply to a training programme, where their need to understand a particular subject is a higher priority than their need to be entertained. But it's still better by far to put the intended information over with a sense of humour, in a way which is likely to keep their interest, however essential it is for them to watch. One of the great advantages of television as a medium is that it can convey facts and stories to people more vividly and more graphically than any other medium — the camcorder which sits so lightly and compactly in the palm of your hand is one of the most powerful communications devices ever invented. But the problem with television as a medium is that it does demand concentration — the audience can't simply turn back to the previous page, as they can when they're reading a book, if they missed something or didn't quite keep up with the explanation which was given.

Another difference between television and non-visual media like radio and the printed word, is that the pictures have to come first. Generally speaking, if a subject can be put over just as well without pictures — or if the pictures themselves are difficult or impossible to produce — then it's better not covered by television. (Having said that, determined and creative producers have succeeded in making memorable television from the most unpromising subjects, against all the odds. But this is still a requirement the beginner needs to bear in mind, to avoid spending a great deal of time on an idea which will probably be both frustrating to shoot and dis-appointing to watch.) Television is also poor at putting over a great mass of detailed information — partly because it would put its audience into a state of information-overload, and partly because it would simply take up too much time. When a novel is adapted for a television play, it has to be drastically reduced to fit the time available — an hour of television drama is directly equivalent to less than a single chapter of a book, which gives an idea of the amount of compression needed to fit the limits of the medium.

This, therefore, gives us a third proviso for our ideas: keep them simple. Programmes made for broadcast purposes — plays, serials and documentaries — often fit into half-hour, forty-five-minute and one-hour or even two-hour slots. Better instead for you to think in terms of ten minutes, or twenty minutes at the outside for a really strong idea. This is far more likely to create the kind of pace which will keep your programme entertaining from start to finish.

Now the most difficult question so far: the subject. Try thinking about any subject you feel really strongly about — something which angers you, or which fascinates you. The chances are you will not only know something about that subject, but the depth of your feelings will suggest a way to communicate those feelings to the audience. However, remember something else too — nothing is more boring to an audience than a one-sided view which they don't happen to share. If you're telling them something which is so important you feel you have to base your programme purely on your own point of view, then be careful to present plenty of evidence to back up your opinion. In all other cases, though, it makes for a better programme to present a roundup of different ideas, opinions and perspectives.

For example, you may be making a programme about motor clubs and the joys of amateur rallying. Everyone involved in it, including yourself, may think it's the greatest sport in the world, but try for a moment to stand back a little from the subject, and look at it objectively. What about people who don't feel so friendly towards the sport? What about people who are kept awake by noisy cars driving fast down country lanes at night? What about people who have been involved in accidents with rally cars? What do the local police think? What are the risks of damage or injury? By including a little of these negative viewpoints to balance the genuine enthusiasms of those who enjoy and support the subject, you'll end up with a more rounded, balanced and entertaining programme.

Another pointer is to look for subjects involving people in one way or another. Programmes about things can still be interesting, but they won't have the universal appeal of people-oriented subjects. People *are* fascinating — whether they're like us, so we can understand and sympathise with their attitudes, their problems, their successes and their failures, or whether they're unlike us, in terms of their spectacular experiences, their criminal actions or their incredible cleverness or bravery.

Figure 21. Some other ideal subjects for a video: a family christening, a wedding, an outdoor meal or the annual holiday.

Good ideas are unpredictable. They can arise almost spontaneously, from a chance word, a line in a newspaper article, or even a reference in a current television or radio programme. They can emerge through lateral thinking — spotting an idea in one particular subject can trigger an idea for a similar look at a closely parallel subject, or even a totally unrelated one. What they usually don't do, is emerge to order. So when a good idea comes to mind, write it down — not necessarily in detail, but in a sufficiently well-described way to help you recall it later, when you have a chance to actually do something with it.

In the end, though, the idea is but the first step on the road to a successful programme. In many cases, it may be the most important requirement: without an original inspiration, many a brilliant programme would never have been made. But in other cases, the idea may be little more than a clearly perceived need: a relative gets married, a child is christened, a house needs to be sold or a visit needs to be preserved on tape. In cases like these, the subject virtually decides itself. But in every case, the next need is for an adequate treatment.

THE RESEARCH

The first stage in producing a treatment is to do the background research. Whether you're making a documentary on a local issue or making a programme on this year's family holiday, you need to investigate the background before you begin. In the first case, what place will you need to visit, and who will you need to talk to, in covering the subject properly? Where can you go for different opinions, and different shades of opinion? What locations and what subjects will give you the most memorable shots? In the second case, what is the destination to be? How will you be getting there, and what scenes and places on the way will give you interesting and varied subjects? What do you expect to do when you get there? Where will you be visiting on sightseeing trips, what activities will you be trying out; in other words, what will you be able to shoot which will interest your audience when the programme is finally completed?

Let's consider one more specific example to see how this works in practice — the documentary on amateur rallying. A first point of approach is to find out which motor clubs in the area actually organise events like this, and when. You'll need the names of some of the drivers who take part, to explain the appeal of the sport, and the names of some of the organisers, to explain how it works, and what the challenges are. You'll need a contact with the local police, to explain their official viewpoint on the conduct of rallies, and the regulations involved. You might well consult local newspaper files to find out names and organisations which have campaigned against the sport in the past, to give you the opposition point of view. Ideally, you need to talk to all these people at the research stage, to gather as much background knowledge of the subject as you can, before you try to build up a treatment.

If research means finding out the subject matter of the programme, drawing up the treatment means specifying how that material is going to be used — it's the outline blueprint of the finished programme. In broad terms, this means thinking in picture sequences, which is where the practice sessions covered in the last chapter come in useful. You'll remember the importance of the recce, when we explained the value of visiting a location for a good look round before you shoot there, even when all we were looking at was a simple story-telling exercise. When planning a properly structured and scripted programme, the recce is even more essential — not just to look at the location itself, but to talk to anyone and everyone who can offer useful advice. These can range from people who can tell you about permission needed for access to attractive camera positions not always available to the general public, to people who can actually take part in the programme itself, as extras or interviewees, or both.

Much of what you look for will depend on the subject of your programme and the kind of location you've chosen. Since trying to cater for any of even the most popular subjects would fill the whole book with vague generalities, or a mass of specific information with too much repetition to be worthwhile, we'll confine ourselves to one working example. It has several advantages which make it an ideal subject for television — colourful and interesting pictures, and a local controversy with issues which can be explained, understood and sympathised with by audiences anywhere in the country.

This is what actually happened. When the railway network was modernised it brought with it the closure of many well-loved, but financially unviable, branch-line routes. But a surprisingly large number of those have been rescued from complete closure, and carefully restored in full operation, as thriving attractions, by a combination of expert professionals and hard-working and enthusiastic amateurs. Many of these projects have become extremely successful, to the point where schemes have been proposed to take over more of the original routes and run services over longer distances — and this is where the trouble begins.

For many of the local people involved, the railway is a welcome and much-loved link with their own past. Many of them worked on it, or travelled on it to school, to their jobs, or on family holidays in the days before widespread car ownership. Seeing it working again, and bringing in visitors by the hundreds of thousands each year, is something which earns their enthusiastic support.

Others have different views. They see the noise and the smoke produced by the steam engines, the smuts on washing and paintwork, the crowds in the shops, the traffic jams and the parking problems in the height of the season. When plans are first announced for the extension of the railway's route and timetables, their reaction is to oppose planning permission, and press for existing services to be curtailed or even abandoned, on grounds ranging from environmental pollution to safety.

The result is that an institution which was originally an important part of a local community is now dividing it, by the very fact of its continued survival and success against all the commercial odds. In at least two cases, during the nineteen seventies and eighties, the success of a restored railway really did produce this kind of controversy. Disagreements simmered below the surface of a happy summertime scene, disagreements which would have astonished most of the visitors who came to enjoy a day out on the source of all this controversy.

In television terms, this makes an ideal subject. The core of the story relates to an activity which provides graphic and colourful picture opportunities. The issues and problems which divide the community into two camps are easy to explain, to understand and to sympathise with. All these factors make it good documentary material, and a useful example with which to explain the details of programme-making, even if your initial preference would be to shoot a series of simple sequences of trains and people as colourfully and vividly as possible.

THE RECCE

So let's begin with the recce, with the intention of making a full documentary on the railway, and the controversy it has provoked among the local people. The initial recce will centre on two areas — places and people. One priority will be to look at the locations along the railway itself which present good shooting possibilities. These might include photogenic scenes, where the railway crosses a picturesque bridge for example, which provide a dramatic background to the colourful spectacle of an immaculately restored locomotive on its way along the line. Other possibilities include glimpses behind the scenes of the reality of running a railway efficiently and professionally, from the interior of a signal box to the locomotive sheds where the engines are cleaned, coaled and watered, ready for their turns of duty.

The second priority relates to the two different kinds of people you need for researching the programme you are trying to make. Some people you need to talk to for information only. Generally speaking, any subject which involves differing opinions and inter-pretations will call for you to talk to a lot of different individuals, to become thoroughly acquainted with the details of the subject, to amass evidence for and against both sides, and search for further leads to new subject matter, and new sources of information.

Secondly, you need to talk to potential interviewees — people who may be part of your list of informa-tion providers, but who have additional qualities which make them worth recording on screen. They may have particularly strong opinions, or they may have a particular story which only they can tell. It's also vital they should be good talkers who can cope with a camera being turned on them — without drying up, at one extreme, or talking too quickly, at the other, so that their contribution becomes a meaningless gabble.

In many cases, your list of interviewees — which will be much shorter than the list of people who are simply providing you with background information — will include suggestions as to where they should be interviewed. If all else fails, you can record them sitting in their own living rooms, but that has three disadvantages. Shooting several interviews in suc-cession, in a series of living rooms, is difficult in terms of supplying enough variety to make the people look interesting and individual. Indoor locations call for more elaborate lighting than outdoor ones. And finally, each interview will carry much more impact if it can be recorded against a background which has some relevance to the story the interviewee is being encouraged to tell.

Let's consider how this would work in the case of our railway subject. Since the railway itself, or the effects it exerts on the community, is the source of the controversy which the programme is covering, then most of the locations will relate to the railway, to the surrounding community, or to both. We'll assume that interviewee A is a volunteer station-master, who is explaining the pleasure which the railway brings to countless visitors of all ages every summer. Interviewee B works on one of the track-maintenance gangs, and wants to describe the hard physical work which goes into keeping the railway running. Interviewee C is a local shopkeeper, worried about trade being driven away by the heavy tourist traffic and the lack of peak-season parking spaces — and Interviewee D is angry at the dirt and noise which the railway brings to their track-side home, especially on days when a full timetable service is being run.

Part of the reason for the recce is to find back-grounds for all these interviews, and others like them. Interviewee A could be interviewed in his office at the station — indeed he (or she) may have to be, if on the day of your shoot the rain is pouring down outside and the station is empty. But on a sunny day, with plenty of people on the platform, the station itself is the ideal background for what A will be talking about — especially if you can pose your interviewee with the crowds and the trains far enough in the background to play a part in the picture, without too much noise from the trains, or waving into the camera by the people, interfering with it.

Interviewee B needs to be questioned beside the track, preferably on a spot where maintenance is going on at the time of the shoot — or can be arranged for the time the interview itself is likely to take place. Similarly, C can be shot beside a crowded street with stationary traffic, or in his or her own shop doorway, or next to a traffic warden putting a ticket on a car which we can assume belongs to one of C's customers. And for D we have two choices — either a seat in the garden, where the trains thundering past only feet away will add weight to what he or she is saying about having them literally on the doorstep, or a shot of the railway itself which emphasises the less attractive features of the iron monsters. A scene where engines are returned to the shed at the end of the day's duty, perhaps, where the fires are dropped and everything is wreathed with smoke rising from grimy heaps of ash, can provide a counterpoint to D's views of the drawbacks of steam power.

Figure 22. Fitting the interview to the background — if the interview is about steam railways being noisy and dirty, then the yard of the engine shed would be an ideal backdrop.

In addition to these two main priorities, the recce offers the chance to check out as many potential problems and opportunities as possible before shooting begins. As before, when we looked at a race meeting, we need to check that we can gain access to the places where interesting viewpoints can be captured on tape. For example, keep your eyes open for places where you can shoot from above or below normal eye level to bring a different perspective to a scene — in railway terms this might mean shooting from bridges over the track, or from below rail level beside embankments.

It may even be possible, by asking the right people and explaining the objectives of your programme, to shoot from signal boxes, locomotive cabs or within the loco shed itself. You can also look along the route of the line to find places where overbridges, under-bridges, or the mouth of a tunnel, will help to provide unusual and dramatic pictures. Look also for other details of railway working, such as the places where engines are replenished with coal and water, or where they're coupled up to the coaches which make up their trains.

At the same time, don't forget people as potential subjects. Apart from your individual employees, you need shots of people turning up in large numbers to enjoy a trip on the line. See if it's possible to shoot from within the booking office, to capture the queues paying the fares for their proposed trips — or visitors in the souvenir shop choosing railway memorabilia, or people packing the platform, or swarming on and off the trains as they pause in the station. Some of the visitors, too, are worth talking to — for a perspective free of the loyalties and priorities which shape the attitudes of the local people we spoke to earlier. Interview them on the train, with all the sights and sounds of the journey in the background. Ask them what they're enjoying most about the day, what they feel about the restoration of the railway, how they'd like to see the route and the service extended, and so on.

Finally, one or two practicalities to bear in mind on the recce. Check the position of the sun at the time you're likely to want to shoot. Some of the shots you want to get may involve shooting directly into the sun and, even with the backlight option on the camera, this will reduce the quality of the footage. Perhaps it's possible to find an alternative shooting position, or to shoot at a different time of day when the sun will have moved across the sky. Look out too for shadows cast by buildings or hills — if your main subject is in deep shadow, that could also cause problems.

Look for the routine of the work which goes on; cleaning and oiling the engines, changing the destination boards at the stations, placing the lamps on the front of the engine, and waving the green flag and blowing the whistle for the train to depart. All these can provide useful cutaways from the main action — as can signals, timetables, posters and nameplates, both on the trains and in the station. Check also for unwanted sounds. Railway sounds are fine, since they relate to the material you're showing in the picture; so engine whistles, the hissing of steam and the squeal of wheels running over points are all all right, except in places where they reach levels which might interfere with your recording of an interview.

Figure 23. Three shots in a sequence of a train leaving — the signal dropping to 'clear', the guard waving the green flag, and the engine passing the station name board.

The real problem arises with noises which don't relate to your subject. If a line-side factory has a loud public-address system, or if visitors on the station platform are playing loud music on portable radios or cassette players, then these sounds won't relate to the scene the audience can see in the picture, and as a result they'll seem louder and more important than they really are. You have two alternatives — shoot a scene with the source of the sound in shot, so the audience is aware afterwards of exactly where it came from, or you can try to avoid the sound altogether. This might mean waiting for it to stop (if it ever *does* stop), asking for it to be stopped while you're shooting, or moving to another part of the location where it becomes less obtrusive.

Finally, use the information you build up on the recce to draw up a shooting plan for the day you come back for the production proper. From this point onwards, we'll assume you have access to one method or another of editing your shots in a different order from that in which you shoot them (more on that later). This means you can finish shooting a particular interview, or at a particular location, before you move on to the next. It also means you can plan your shooting day to take variables like weather into account. For example, if you know from the weather forecast that it's likely to be clear and sunny in the morning but turn to rain and low cloud in the afternoon, then you can plan to shoot all the critical fair-weather material in the morning, leaving the rest for later in the day. But bear two more points in mind: the weather may change in a different sequence from that predicted by the official forecasters, and you need to keep the requirements of continuity in mind. Two shots which will be edited together, one after the other, in the finished programme, shouldn't be shot in vastly different weather and lighting conditions. Brilliant sunshine to pouring rain in the fraction of a second taken for a single picture cut won't be convincing. On the other hand, there will be times when you can use a lighting or weather change in a particular scene to emphasise the passing of time — fading out from a street corner on a sunny midday and fading in again on the same street corner in the low sunlight of evening, for example, tells the audience that several hours have passed, without the need for an additional shot to emphasise the fact.

We also need to check the order of events on the day you will be shooting — in our specific example, this means consulting the train timetable above all. When you're set up on a particular bridge waiting for a train to appear, you want to know more or less how long you need to wait. You can also check how much warning you have, from the noise of the engine whistle, or the plume of smoke wafting above the trees, when a train *is* on its way to you. Take particular note of the times of the last train of the day. If you still need to secure train footage as that time approaches, it will have to take top priority — you can always cope with the final interviews and some of the cutaways after the trains have stopped running.

Finally, let us consider the possibility of covering a subject which is less under our control than this example. Apart from the running times of the trains, the order in which the interviews are recorded, the people we talk to and the questions we ask are matters of choice. But if you set out instead to shoot an event with a particular, set sequence of actions which will take place in that order and with that timing, whether you're there or not, then the recce has to do a slightly different job.

The most familiar example of this type of assignment is covering a christening or, especially, a wedding. But it can also apply to school prize-givings, the opening of a local factory, office or shopping development, or the presentation of a retirement gift to a long-serving member of a company's staff. It can apply to a children's nativity play, to amateur dramatics or to a local concert. In all these cases, you need to see as detailed and faithful a replica of the event itself as you can, in time to plan your shooting. If you're able to shoot the last night of an event which runs on several successive evenings, then a recce on the first night may tell you what you need to

Figure 24. Any event which follows a set schedule — from a choir recital to an impromtu singsong — will be easier to cover if you carry out a recce beforehand.

know. Otherwise you may have to go to the dress rehearsal or, if this doesn't give you sufficient warning or if there isn't going to *be* a rehearsal as such, then you need to talk to the planners of the event for the information you seek. And don't forget — if they can't tell you exactly what will happen because they themselves haven't yet done their planning homework, then any help you can give — which will, incidentally, make your job easier and more rewarding — will probably be gratefully received!

CHAPTER FOUR

A SUITABLE CASE FOR TREATMENT

The previous chapter dealt with finding a subject, and organising the research and reconnaissance needed to plan the way in which it will be shot. But programme production is a complex process, and these different stages don't always happen in a set order of individual, complete steps, each one of which has to be finished before the next can begin. In this chapter, we're going to look at the process of turning the original idea into a planned programme treatment. Part of the information which helps to develop that treatment will result from the research and the recce, but frequently the two processes may go on side-by-side — so closely, in fact, that it's difficult always to be certain of a dividing line between one and the other.

A specific example might make this slightly clearer. In our local-railway documentary example, some of the decisions governing the treatment of the subject would have to be taken early enough to influence the recce. One instance is the assumption that was made over the intention to interview people of different opinions against suitable backgrounds on location — most of them at different places along the railway itself. Because of the decision, part of the recce was devoted to finding and assessing those particular places — but had the treatment not specified shooting footage of the railway to give the background information for the programme, but instead to assemble all the different interviewees at a neutral location to record the arguments, interactions and differences of opinion between them, then this stage of the recce would definitely not have been necessary.

What usually happens in reality, then, is a combination of both processes at once. The initial outline plan for the programme is part of the development of the treatment, but this needs research to take it beyond more than a mere statement of intent. Until we know *what* we're covering, *who* we can talk to and *where* we can shoot, we can't plan a recce to move us on to the next stage of making the programme. The answers to these questions will help decide the ultimate shape of the programme well before the treatment proper is drawn up. And decisions as to whether the subject is covered on location or in the studio, with a dramatised or a factual approach, and whether to use an on-screen presenter or a voice-over commentary to reinforce the pictures and link the interviews, will be imposed by the type of subject and your own resources more than they will by purely creative drives.

Now let's concentrate on the treatment proper, assuming that we either have the information we need to take the necessary decisions at this stage, or that we can carry out the investigations and recces in parallel with the development of the treatment. We know, to revert to our example, that we have the basic story line, the location — in general terms — and the people to whom we shall be talking for the whole range of opinions, attitudes, experiences and wishes we want to include in the programme. At this stage there is an enormous variety of ways in which that information can be put over on the screen, without even considering the formidable battery of weapons which even an amateur programme-maker can use to reinforce the impact of the programme — graphics, special effects, library material and music to name just four. All of them will be covered in later chapters, so for the time being we shall assume that the treatment will be confined to a straightforward documentary, here-and-now approach, with the addition of a few simple historic and graphic effects we shall cover in greater detail as the treatment proceeds. But there are still decisions to be made before the planning can go much further.

OPENING WITH IMPACT

Again, the easiest way to describe what's involved is by example. Taking the opening section of the programme, we want to seize our audience's attention as powerfully as we can. Generally speaking, that won't be done by showing talking heads — people giving us their views, however varied, just by sitting in a chair and talking to an unseen questioner. In certain circumstances (like, for example, having stumbled across evidence of a monumental crime, or having made a miraculous and incredible escape from a terrible disaster) the impact of the words can be enormously powerful. So powerful, indeed, that in these few cases, the understatement of the talking-head picture can be very successful in allowing the words to speak for themselves. But that's *not* likely in this case — what we have here are people with something interesting to say, rather than a story so unique as to seize the audience with the simple power of its words.

So we take our first decision. We need a dramatic opening sequence of pictures, which tell the audience something about the subject of our programme, but leave enough unsaid to intrigue them and make them want to learn more. This might be a shot of a tunnel mouth, with a few wisps of smoke curling upwards from the archway — accompanied by the roar of an approaching train. After a few seconds of suspense, with the noise growing louder and louder, the train bursts forth into the light with colour, noise, steam and movement, before we cut to the next shot in the sequence.

Another alternative might be to look for a spot where a long straight stretch of track gives way to a sharp curve. By siting the camera on a tripod as closely as possible to the bend (provided permission can be obtained or a public viewpoint found) and using the full zoom lens to foreshorten and magnify the image of the approaching train as far as possible, it's easy to produce a very dramatic image. On the one hand, you have the threatening sight of a

Figure 25. Two possibilities for more dramatic shots — the static subject of the dark tunnel mouth is made more threatening by the roar of the train as it approaches without being seen, and the close-up of the engine seen on the very end of the zoom is obviously moving very fast, though the size of the image on the screen only grows very slowly and deliberately.

powerful locomotive apparently heading straight for the camera (especially if the combination of your camera position, and the zoom of your lens, allows you to hide the fact that the rails curve safely away before they reach you). On the other, the wisps of steam, the noise and the blur of wheels and pistons show the train is travelling quickly, yet all that happens is that the front of the locomotive grows slowly larger in the frame — the foreshortening of distance which occurs at the telephoto end of the zoom lending a dramatic and dream-like quality to the shot.

Having decided for the sake of our example on the second approach, since this allows a longer opening shot and a heightening of the tension, we now need to decide what the sound should do to back the picture. The sound of the approaching train is one option — the level climbing slowly as the train moves nearer and nearer to the camera. The use of music as an additional effect, to heighten the impact of the oncoming train, is another. But both these effects can be used at the beginning of the shot, leaving it possible to add the opening words of the script before the shot is over, to carry on under the following shots in the opening sequence, and lead us and the audience into the programme proper.

TREATMENT OPTIONS

But what should those opening words be? At this stage we are not trying to pre-empt the writing of the full script, all we need to know is roughly what will be said so that the treatment can be developed. In basic terms, we have three possible options which will set the scene for three slightly differing approaches to the subject. If we want to establish the idea in the minds of the audience from the start, that this is a familiar and well-loved scene — and only then to tell them that beneath this image of nostalgia and enjoyment lie deep and bitter feelings among a whole section of the local community, then one option open to us is to spell that out very deliberately with a section of voice-over commentary.

Let's look first at how that would appear on the page. The first step in drawing up a treatment proper is to set out the programme sequence by sequence, with the pictures summarised in the left-hand column, and the sounds (sound effects, music or words), down the right-hand column. Where a section of the commentary in the right-hand column is related directly to a particular sequence of pictures in the left-hand column, then as far as possible the two pieces of description should be level on the page. In this way, it's possible to have a clear idea about how the programme treats the subject from the opening shot to the closing titles. And the very act of drawing up a document like this is an aid to concentrating the mind — it will reveal without fail any area where your thinking hasn't been developed sufficiently, or if more work on the pictures, or the words, needed for a particular section, must be done to produce a coherent shape for the programme.

But it doesn't have to be done in great detail, you don't have to write all the words, or even all the questions for the interviews. All these will come later. In picture terms, you don't need to specify the programme shot by shot. Sequence headings will give enough information for this stage of the programme, though if any particularly unusual shots or inputs are planned, then it may help to refer to them very briefly at the appropriate point in the layout. For our first approach, the treatment will begin something like this:

TROUBLE ON THE LINE	OUTLINE TREATMENT
PICTURES:	SOUND:
1. Dramatic opening shot of approaching train through telephoto at Whitchurch Curve.	Sound effects and music. Commentary begins: Picture from the past on the Little Snoring Railway. Colour and spectacle of old steam trains — remarkable feat of restoration.
2. Shots on station — happy holiday crowds.	Yesterday's working railway now magnet for visitors — many of them

too young to remember real steam railway of past. But behind scenes, not everyone is so happy about what is going on . . .

3. Interviewee A. Background of loco shed.	'Steam trains nasty smelly things — thought we'd seen the last of them — why do they have to bring them back?'
4. Interviewee B. Background of jammed traffic in busy street.	'All these visitors to the railway don't do anything for trade — can't get through town on days when railway's running — people can't park near shops, trade's dropped right off . . .'
5. Sequence in booking office with queue waiting for tickets.	But for visitors themselves, no doubts at all . . .
6. Family waiting for train.	Vox pop quotes — what people enjoy about the railway.
7. Stationmaster on platform.	For volunteers like John so-and-so; this is culmination of years of hard work.
8. Stationmaster interview.	'Determined not to let old line die . . . whole community would have been poorer for its loss . . . meant years of struggle, to raise the money and repair the damage . . . all has been worthwhile in the end . . . just look around at how people are enjoying it . . .'

As a very rough rule of thumb, we ought to allow around four separate points to be made for each minute of programme time. This means that sequence 1, with the approaching train, needs to be on-screen for around thirty seconds to establish the two main points, plus say another 15 seconds for the picture, the sound effects and the music to become properly established at the opening of the programme, giving us a total of around three-quarters of a minute in all. For sequences 2 and 3, we're looking at another 45 seconds each, with another minute for sequence 4, and another 15 seconds for sequence 5. All this adds up to around three-and-a-half minutes of programme time — though, in order not to swamp the pictures with words, the commentary and interview quotes shouldn't take up more than around two to two-and-a-half minutes of this time.

For sequence 6, the vox-pop quotes, this depends on the number of answers you include. Vox pop is short for 'vox populi', Latin for 'voice of the people'. In broadcast terms, it's used to describe interviews with members of the public who don't have a formal, individual identification with the subject of the programme. Usually their quotes are included to give an idea of the public mood on an issue, or of the range of opinions on more controversial matters. As a general rule, three quotes is a large enough number to suggest a consensus of opinion, if what they say is broadly in agreement with one another. If you find a wide variation in what people say in answer to your questions, you may need more. But vox-pop interviews are a specialised technique we'll cover in more detail later on. For the time being, we're only working them into the treatment outline.

Sequence 7 adds another fifteen seconds, with the stationmaster interview accounting for between sixty and seventy-five seconds more. This means that setting the scene, and giving an idea of the different points of view people have about the railway which is the subject of our programme, has taken a total of up to five minutes — which, in programme terms, is quite a long time. And it's also a fairly conventional treatment in that the story develops along rather obvious lines, with the surprise element fairly muted.

How can we go about changing this emphasis? Suppose we start with the same opening shot, but instead of reinforcing the mood with an introductory section of commentary, we go straight into the direct quotes from our interviewees. In that case our treatment might start like this:

TROUBLE ON THE LINE	OUTLINE TREATMENT
1. Telephoto shot of approaching train, seen head-on from Whitchurch Curve.	Sound effects and music. Different voices then supply quotes from interviews dealt with in more detail later:

'Steam engines — nasty smelly things, why did they have to bring them back?'

'The whole line's a remarkable achievement — years of hard work to get it working again — look how everyone's enjoying it'

'Doesn't do a thing for trade — crowds of visitors — nowhere to park — business has dropped off sharply . . .'

With a single shot, this version of the treatment has established a railway location (though not necessarily *which* railway) and a degree of controversy in around half the time it took us in the previous version. But is the story line strong enough? There is a possibility that the contrasting views, coming in as voices over that shot, might not produce a strong enough theme on which to begin. Perhaps it might be worth prolonging the shot by using it to its full length, but cutting backwards and forwards to it, and in the meantime seeing a brief glimpse of each of our interviewees to establish them as individuals.

We can also begin with the image of the train as an oncoming, slightly threatening image, and use this to reinforce the negative quotes first, so it seems as if the programme is taking a particular point of view. But once this point of view is established, we can then introduce the positive aspects of the line's restoration and commercial success, and some of the quotes from those responsible for the success. In treatment terms, this third approach might look more like the following version.

TROUBLE ON THE LINE	OUTLINE TREATMENT
1. Telephoto shot of approaching train, seen head-on from Whitchurch Curve.	Sound effects and music.
2. Shot of first interviewee in loco shed yard.	'Steam engines — nasty, dirty, smelly things — why bring them back?'
3. Cut back to approaching train, this time recognisably closer.	
4. Shot of second interviewee by shop doorway.	'Doesn't do a thing for trade — crowds of visitors — nowhere to park — business has dropped off sharply . . .'
5. Return to approaching shot, train closer still, larger and more threatening. And so on . . .	

THE TREATMENT AS A BLUEPRINT

For the first few minutes of our proposed programme, we've explored three different styles of treatment. Each of them could be equally valid as a start to the programme, with a balance of advantages and drawbacks. In the end, though, as you work through from the beginning of the programme to the conclusion, the treatment you develop will tell you several indispensable things about the way you plan your production. It will, for a start, show you whether your original idea is strong enough to sustain an entire programme as it stands, or whether it needs more input.

For example, there may be a place in your treatment for a short historical sequence on how and why the railway first came to be built, and when it was closed. Illustrating this may be a problem, as there is unlikely to be much in the way of archive film you could work into your programme. But the local library, or the local newspaper, may be able to produce still pictures or press cuttings of the railway (not to mention people who actually worked on the line), all of which can be used as graphics to be included in your programme.

For broadcast producers, who have a definite gap in the schedule to fill (called a 'slot', usually 15, 20, 30, 45 or 60 minutes long) the programme length has to fit precisely. Even for amateur programme-makers, with no definite running-time requirement to meet, it's useful to have a target length in mind. And the best way to hit this target is to make sure your treatment adds up to your target running time plus, say, a 20 per cent margin. In most cases, it's easy to take material out of a programme by trimming sequences and tightening up the script and interviews, and in most cases the programme will be better for it. Adding new material to fill a gap is much less satisfactory.

The treatment also helps ensure you haven't left anything out. But it can do a great deal more than that. By keeping it to hand as an essential blueprint for the programme as a whole, it can help you to respond to the inevitable changes which occur as the production continues. Sometimes shots, or interviews, can be disappointing — or they can reveal many more facets to the story which cry out to be explored and, often, to be included in the programme. If you have a working treatment, you can try out the effects of these alterations, so that links can be changed, and even the order in which the sequences will be edited together, to make the best use of the new material. But you will still have an accurate idea of the effect on the overall running time, and on the shape of the programme which will result.

For professional programme-makers, the treatment has two more crucial parts to play. It allows you to turn the making of the programme into shooting days, travelling days and editing days to allow you to draw up a schedule and a budget for the whole production. In cases where the programme is being made for a client who wants bids from a number of potential producers, then very often the treatment is the document which decides whether you, or one of your competitors, actually wins the job of making the programme. And what could be more important in the whole production process than that?

CHAPTER FIVE

LET SHOOTING COMMENCE

At last you feel happy with your subject, your treatment, your recce and your background research. The great day arrives, when you can go out and begin shooting with a definite programme in mind. This is the time when you have to adjust your approach to look at your subject from a different perspective. For most of the planning process, you will have been working as a researcher, as a producer and as a scriptwriter — now you have to switch back to looking at your surroundings with the eye of a director and a camera operator.

As we explained earlier on, we are assuming for shooting purposes that the programme can be edited later — either by linking camera and VCR for assemble and insert editing, by using one of the new home-video edit controllers now on the market, or by hiring a professional edit suite, with or without editor. This will be explained in more detail in the chapter covering editing (for many people the most challenging and fascinating area of programme production), but for the time being, what matters is that this assumption will have two effects on our shooting methods.

The first is that, clearly, we don't have to shoot material in the order in which we want to use it. This makes an enormous difference to the freedom and the efficiency of shooting, in that — as mentioned earlier — we can shoot all the sequences involving a particular contributor or a particular location at the same session, wherever these sequences may be used in the finished programme. On the other hand, this does mean that each sequence must be coded and identified, so it's easy to tell exactly where it has to fit in the final programme. And that means a little more planning before we start.

TAGGING YOUR TAKES

Sometimes programmes are made to a full and detailed script before shooting starts. If this includes not only every word of commentary, but also every single shot, then coding the shots as they are recorded is very easy. If shot 196 in the script is a zoom back from a signal to the train waiting to depart, then the camera will be set up to record precisely that shot, and the shot will be identified as 'Shot 196, take 1'. In the days of shooting on film, this was done with a clapperboard, with the number of the shot and the take chalked on it. This was held up in front of the camera at the start of the shot, and the camera assistant would read out 'shot 196, take 1' before slamming the jaws of the clapperboard shut. The noise of the jaws closing on the soundtrack tape could then be lined up with the frame of the film which showed the jaws closing together, so the film and soundtrack could be synchronised before starting to edit the sequences together.

Video, unlike film, doesn't carry picture and sound information on separate tapes, so that the synchronisation problem doesn't arise. It's still a good idea to identify your shots in the picture though. If you precede each shot by holding up a board in front of the camera with the number of the shot and the take chalked on it (no need for clappers here), then it's easy to spot when you may be winding through a tape on fast-search looking for a particular shot. You won't hear the soundtrack, but a brief glimpse of the board as you wind through the tape at speed is usually enough to tell you when it's time to stop to catch a particular shot.

The take number is the number of the attempt you're making to capture that particular shot. If you get it right first time, then one take is all you need. But you'll often find that an unexpected sound at the wrong moment, or someone waving at the camera, or an unwanted wobble of the tripod, can spoil the take for one reason or another. You then need to do the shot again, identifying it as 'shot 196, take 2' and so on, until you get it right.

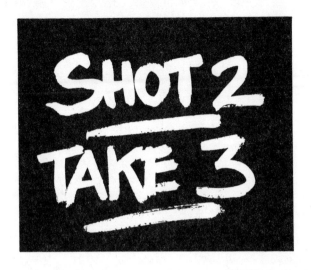

Figure 26. A chalk board held in front of the camera to identify the shot, and the take, is a great help during editing.

Of course, you may not have a completely detailed script to work from. Another approach is to identify each shot by the number of the sequence in the treatment into which it's supposed to fit. If sequence 15 has an opening shot of an engine taking on water in the station, then this shot may be tagged shot 15/1, take 1. If the second shot in the sequence is a close-up of the fireman opening the filler cap on the tender, then this becomes shot 15/2, and so on. Finally, it's also possible to drop all reference to the treatment or script, and just number your shots in order as you record them. But in that case, you'll need an extra-detailed cross-reference scheme in your shot lists to keep track of the areas of the script being covered as shooting continues.

The other half of the shot-tagging process is the shot list itself. On a professional crew, this is kept by the production assistant, or PA, whose job includes logging every take in the order in which it's recorded. As each tape is used up, it acquires a list of all the shots contained on it, with their takes and durations, and a list of remarks to identify which are the best takes and which takes are likely to offer compromises at the edit stage. For example, an unwanted noise late in a take might not prevent it from being used, if a cutaway allows it to be combined with a different take, with a clear soundtrack, for the later part of the shot.

While you may be doing all these jobs yourself, it probably isn't necessary to keep such a detailed record. But it takes little longer to label each shot properly, and even when you don't have time — because events may be moving too quickly — then *anything* you can remember once you have a chance to pause and jot down some notes, is more useful than trying to recollect the details some days or weeks later, when you're playing back the tape before editing. Even a note of which take seemed best at the time may be helpful — though you may find on playback that noises and camera movements which seemed distracting at the time don't matter so much from the viewer's point of view.

Where an interview is being recorded, the shot list needs to be more detailed. Each question put to the interviewee should be written down, even if the reading of the question itself isn't being recorded at this stage. We'll take a closer look at interviews later, but for the time being it's worth noting that the first and last words of each answer, *or* (if you're having to make notes yourself as well as operate the camera) the broad theme of the interviewee's response, should be jotted down with an estimate of how far into the tape it was recorded and, if you can, an idea of how long the answer lasted.

WORKING TO A ROUTINE

Now to the shooting itself. With experience, you will find it simpler to cover a particular section of the story from keeping track of the different shots — long shot, medium shot, close-up — which you record of each subject. You will find yourself shifting camera position and angle to produce a new perspective, and altering framing and movement almost by instinct. But until you become this skilled at thinking on the move, and shooting a subject from memory without leaving any gaps — which only emerge when you arrive back home and play back the tape in full — it's better by far to work to a routine.

Figure 27. Starting and finishing a moving shot: as the train starts to move and approaches your camera position, pan with it by concentrating on a single focus of interest — either a nameplate or (as here) the driver's cab. When the pan is finished, keep the camera steady, and let the train carry on out of the frame.

First of all, let us consider the part of the action which may be under your control. Let's use that

example of the railway engine taking on water —
what actually happens? The engine reverses up to
the water tank, the fireman climbs down from the
cab, walks back to the rear end of the tender, pulls
the water-tank hose across, and then climbs up the
steps onto the top of the tender. When he reaches
the top, he opens the filler cap, pushes the water
hose into the filler pipe, then pulls a chain or rope to
start the water pouring into the tank. So, begin by
moving far enough back to capture the whole process in long shot, and shoot it from start to finish.
Simple. This is your master shot.

Now you need to consider your alternative shots.
Depending on the level of cooperation you can look
for from the engine crew, you may be able to
persuade them to go through the routine several
times for the benefit of the camera. If so, then you
can set up beside the track for a medium shot of the
engine backing towards you, and the fireman
climbing down and walking towards the cameras,
before he climbs out of frame up the tender steps. Or
you may be able to position yourself on top of the
tender, so you see the fireman walking from above,
and when he climbs the steps to join you on top of
the tender, you can see the opening of the filler cap
and the loading of the hose in close-up.

The possibilities are almost limitless, provided that
you, and the people you are shooting, have enough
time. With increasing experience, you will look at
things with a skilled eye and pick only those shots
which are particularly unusual, well-framed or illuminating. Or you may find that, while the engine
crew are willing to help, other reasons mean they
cannot move the engine once it has stopped by the
water tank. In cases like this, you have to think, and
move, more quickly. Go for your master shot as
before. Then ask them to pause while you set up for
a medium shot of the fireman walking towards you,
and then ask them to pause again, while you climb
up on top of the tender, and then give the fireman
the cue to climb up towards you and carry on with
the rest of his routine. As an extra insurance, you

could then go back to ground level and ask him to do the tail end of the drill — opening the filler cap, and so forth again, so you have the same process from two different perspectives.

This is where continuity comes in. Wherever possible, try to make sure your subject does the same actions in the same order and at the same speed, whenever you shoot him. This is another area where you need to concentrate very closely on what's happening. Ask yourself afterwards, did he use his left hand or his right hand to open the filler cap, his left hand or right hand to pull on the rope? Did he turn round from one task to the next, or did he take a couple of steps as well? Did he pause at any time, to give a gap in the action — and did he look back at the camera to check you'd shot what you needed? All these things need checking, and your subject may not even be aware of changing hands or movements between one run-through of an absolutely routine task and the next. But *you* need to know —it's far easier to point out a change, if you've spotted it, and ask for another go, than it will be to cope with continuity problems at the editing stage.

This same routine will guide you through most of the sequences in the story. Start each new location with a wide shot, which will provide a master for the entire set of sequences taking place on that location. Where you intend to shoot an interview, try if you can to shoot a sequence of your interviewee doing something connected with the subject of the interview, but not on the same spot. For example, before interviewing the stationmaster, try to record some shots of him walking round the station talking to visitors, checking the timetable, watching the departure of a train, and so on. Where you're about to shoot an interview with a shopkeeper, show him behind the counter talking to customers, or anything else which relates to what he's going to say in the interview. This additional material will be worth its weight in diamonds when it comes to editing the interview.

Another point to bear in mind when doing this: you sometimes need an introductory shot to smooth your way into the interview, and one of these shots will be ideal — provided your subject moves out of the frame at the end. So make sure you have at least one shot where this happens, and preferably more to give you a greater choice. A secondary insurance is to keep looking out for possible cutaway shots which can be used almost anywhere in the programme. A distant shot of a train pulling out of the station, or simply running through the countryside; a shot of a station clock — making sure the time it shows is appropriate — or a timetable; advertisements and station signs; people waiting for trains or crossing the station footbridge; signals, whether at 'clear' or at 'danger', or (especially) changing from one to the other. All these are ideal for cutaways, and can be used in different places to punctuate the main action or guard against jump cuts when shots are being edited.

Sometimes you will be shooting an interviewee while he or she is working. If so, you may need to shoot a close-up of them pressing a button or flicking through some papers or stirring a cup of coffee, to give you additional cutaways. Even when someone is not being interviewed, you may still need close-up cutaways of some parts of the action — such as the signalman pressing the bell in the signal box to pass a message to his colleagues further down the line. By shooting this again in close-up, you give yourself more freedom over the shot you use next, when later trying to edit for speed and brevity.

Another useful dodge, for when you're shooting a scene which is reasonably static, but essential to your story, is to give yourself the maximum choice between a long shot and a close-up. You simply record the shot as a zoom-in, and then as a zoom-out, leaving at least three seconds at either end of the zoom. You can then use that shot in four different ways — long shot, close-up, zoom-in or zoom-out — as long as you only choose one of the options. It's also worth considering the POV (point-of-view) shot. Broadly speaking, this results from putting the camera in the position of the person we have just been watching. If you've just shot a horse-drawn wagon pulling up in the station yard, see if it's possible for you to sit next to the driver while he repeats the manoeuvre — then you can shoot it as if the camera were seeing the scene through the driver's eyes. These POV shots can have a very powerful visual appeal, if they're used sparingly.

Reaction shots are a slightly different version of the same approach. We've already referred to one, when speaking of shooting the fireman starting his climb to the tender top from ground level, then moving to the tender top to shoot him finishing his climb. This is a reaction shot, though we didn't identify it as such, because we are looking back at the action from the opposite direction. Another example would be when shooting a railwayman climbing down from the platform in between the engine and the coaches to hook them up together. If you could follow a shot of him climbing down into the gap, by a shot *from* the gap of him doing the same thing, this could provide a neat and attractive cut. Again, keep it simple and don't use the effect too often.

CROSSING THE LINE

When using reaction shots, however, there's a classic problem of film and television shooting which has to be borne in mind. It's long been a cardinal rule that you have to establish a line along which the action takes place, and then you have to take care to stay on one side of it. If, for example, we want to cover the journey of a train down the line, then we need to be sure we always stay on the same side of the tracks so that, whatever our shot, the train is — broadly speaking — moving in the same direction. If the sequence builds up with the train always moving from left to right, then if we cut at any point to a shot of it moving from right to left, the audience will find it confusing and distracting. We will have 'crossed the line', and the picture will imply that the train has decided to reverse its direction and head back the way it came. The same thing can happen in interviews — if you cross the line, it can look as if the interviewer and interviewee have changed places.

We'll look at this again when we cover interviews in more detail. For the time being, it's worth being aware of the problem and trying to avoid crossing the line through ignorance and thoughtlessness. In some circumstances you can get away with it quite legitimately but, if at all in doubt, it's better to record a few extra shots to help you solve the problem. Returning to our example of the passing train, if you take care to shoot at least one setup with the train coming straight towards the camera (from an over-bridge across the line would be ideal) then you can cut to another shot of the train from the other side of the line without it being too confusing. But don't cross the line more than you have to, or the result may still be messy and confusing in the end.

Figure 28. All these pictures of different cars in a procession of classic transport can be edited in a logical sequence because the camera is always looking at them from the same side of the road. If, however, one of the shots had been from the opposite side of the road (crossing the line) it would have given the impression that particular subject was going the other way, and spoiled the procession sequence by confusing the audience.

How much should you shoot to ensure you have enough material? If you shoot twice as much tape as the length of your programme, you *may* have enough to edit it to the planned length. Four to one is a better ratio, as this gives you more chance to avoid shots which, for one reason or another, are less than ideal. If you find yourself using more tape than this to begin with, don't worry. At least it shows you are taking pains with the material. With increasing experience you may find you are using less, or you may become increasingly ambitious and critical of your own efforts, and actually use more. The standard of programme which results is the final justification for the tape you use.

Instead of overall tape consumption, it's probably a better idea to keep a check on how much tape you devote to different areas of shooting: scripted shots, interview material and all the 'covering' shots (insurance views of scenes, cutaways for interviews and the like). Ideally, you won't go far wrong if your programme material is made up half of the first category, and around a quarter each of the second and third. But much will depend on the character and subject-matter of the programme, and in any case this balance can vary from day to day. It's better to run an occasional check through the material you collect over several days of shooting, to verify you have the balance about right.

CHAPTER SIX

THROWING MORE LIGHT ON THE SUBJECT

Shooting on location — outdoor location that is — does pose certain problems. Bad weather, extraneous noise, access to what you want to cover, can all come between you and your subject. But outdoor shooting does usually minimise one potential problem: lighting your subject properly. The word, however, was chosen carefully. Outdoor shooting may 'minimise' the lighting problem. It *doesn't* eliminate it entirely.

LIGHTING AND EXTERIOR SHOOTS

Take the ideal conditions for outdoor shooting: a bright sunny day, with no irritating clouds to change the light level in the middle of a shot, or pose continuity problems if the sun dives behind a big cloud bank when you're ready to shoot the subject from a different angle. For your long shots, you may find that the sunshine washing over the whole scene tends to flatten it and take the depth out of the landscape. The way to avoid this is to look for patches of shadows, and changes in the camera position and angle, to find a combination of light and shade in the background and enough interest in the foreground to put that quality of depth back into the picture.

Modern camcorders, with their backlight facility, have made it possible to shoot in the direction of the sun — though not directly at it — without a total picture washout. But it's true that you will still find better pictures shooting with the sun to one side of you, or behind you. Remember, too, that many commercials are shot in the early morning or late evening — not just because it may be quieter then, but because the lower light gives more depth to the picture.

In most cases, shooting outdoors means making the best of what you have. You can't change the position of the sun in the sky, except by waiting a long time to shoot a scene. So unless the problem of into-the-sun shooting can be solved by going away and shooting something else, returning a few hours later when the sun has moved round the sky, you have to do the best you can. Watch out for bright patches and shadows, and use them to balance the picture. Avoid brilliant reflections from white walls or bright metal, unless they give you the effect you are looking for. Make use of shadows where they help add depth to the picture — but there are places where these too can be troublesome.

Imagine an interview conducted in bright sunshine. Because of the need to pose your interviewee in a particular direction, so as to show part of the background in the frame, you may find their forehead is in shot, but the bottom part of the face is in deep shadow. In cases like these, professional crews would use lights, even in broad daylight, to damp out unwanted shadows. But you can avoid this by recruiting someone to help you, and giving them a sheet of reflecting material. By experimenting with its position relative to the sun and to the subject, you can use it to kill unwanted shadows *without* the need for extra equipment. Screens and umbrellas which reflect light can be bought from photographic accessory shops — or you can make your own by stretching sheets of kitchen foil over a light framework a couple of feet square.

LIGHTING AND INTERIOR SHOOTS

All of these considerations pale into insignificance, though, compared with the demands of shooting indoors, when lighting really does come into its own. The reason for this is that, for all the amazing advances in modern camcorder performance, which includes response to low light levels, they're still a long way behind the human eye. We can adapt to indoor light levels far below the conditions existing out of doors, without really being aware of it. Camcorders have a much more difficult time coping with subdued lighting. When video cameras were based on tubes, then any bright patch in the picture left a trail across the frame whenever the camera moved. The picture looked dark and fuzzy, and the depth of field was so short that this added to the out-of-focus feel of the shot. Even those circuits which were intended to boost low-light performance also increased the 'noise' in the picture, so the effect was that of a normal television broadcast subject to added interference.

Today's cameras are much better in these conditions. But it's still worth lighting an indoor scene properly, since the picture quality, even with the most sophisticated model, will improve by leaps and bounds if it's properly lit. What the improved low-light performance means is that existing light can do more of the work than it used to — all we have to consider is where that light needs to be boosted to give us the kind of picture we want. Let's begin with the relatively simple task of lighting a single face, either an interviewee responding to questions, or a presenter speaking to camera.

Figure 29. The basic lighting layout for one person talking to camera: the key light (lower right), the filler light (lower left) and the back light (top left).

116

Sometimes news crews, working against the clock with a minimum of equipment, will lift the available light with an extra light of their own, mounted on or near the camera and shining directly at the subject. This does make the face more discernible, especially if shooting in really poor light, but it has two major disadvantages for picture quality. Because the light is falling from beside the camera, it tends to flatten the face into a bright disc against the dark background. And unless the background is fairly well lit too, it can become so indistinct that its picture value is lost altogether.

The main light we need for good results is called the 'key' light, set up to illuminate the subject from one side of the picture or the other at an angle to the camera. If the subject is facing the camera, as a presenter, then the key light can be on either side. If the subject is an interviewee facing an off-screen questioner to the right of the frame, then the key light should be placed to the camera operator's right, to reduce the shadow thrown by the subject's nose across the cheek. The height is also critical — it needs to be above the eyeline of the subject and above the camera, but not too high as it would then tend to cast shadows from the eyebrows.

You can find the right position for the key light with a little trial and error. First of all, set the light up just above and behind the camera, shining directly on your subject. You'll find that your subject's face looks flat and two-dimensional, with all the shadows and details washed out, and with a slightly disembodied appearance, as it floats in front of a large pool of shadow cast on the wall behind.

Now try moving the light away from the camera — still pointing it carefully at the subject — and check the effects of each move on the picture showing on the screen. As the light moves away from the camera at a wider angle, the features of the face will appear more and more three-dimensional, as the shadows cast by nose and eyebrows become more marked, and the shadow on the wall behind the subject disappears to one side. If you ask your subject to look to the side of the camera on which you've placed the light — as they would in a studio interview, for example — you can avoid the shadow cast by the nose being too prominent, while still producing the three-dimensional effect of a real face rather than a flat photograph. In the same way, changing the height of the lamp can reduce the shadows cast by the eyebrows over the eye sockets, which might otherwise look too dark and mysterious.

When the light is in the right position you will find a very powerful image on the screen, with one half of the face (or thereabouts) brilliantly lit, and the other half in deep shadow. This is the kind of dramatic effect — called chiaroscuro, from the Italian for 'bright-dark' — exploited by many of the world's greatest painters. The problem, for our purposes, is that it's a shade *too* dramatic — fine for a scene from a horror movie or murder mystery, or a shot at a moment of tension in a play. But for a normal interview we need a second light to soften the contrast between the areas of light and dark in the face, to bring it closer to what our own eyes would see.

As a comparison, look directly at your subject's face. You will see the bright areas clearly enough, but unless the light is too bright for its job, you'll also see the shadowed portions of the face in some detail. Less bright perhaps, but not as black as the picture on the screen, which is limited by the range of contrast which the camera can cope with. So once again, we have to use a light to make the camera's job — of standing in for the human eye — a little bit easier, and a great deal more possible.

Where the first light is called the key light, the second light is called the 'filler', which describes its job fairly well. It needs to be placed where it can fill in those areas of shadow and hint at the substance of the face — what it must *not* do is rival the intensity of the key light, or we would regress to the beginning, with a flat, two-dimensional face with even illumi-

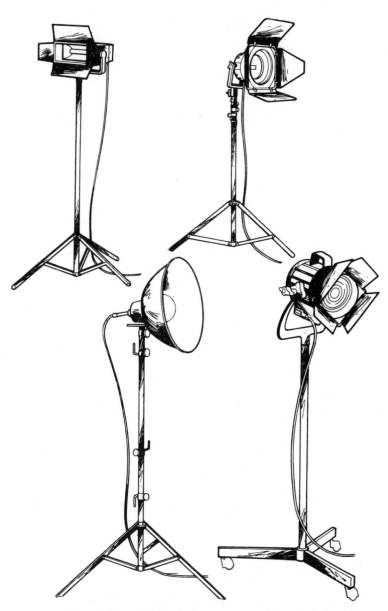

Figure 30. Types of lights: the linear-type quartz halogen light (top left) gives a wide, high-output beam, while the cheaper photoflood (bottom left) is useful for wide-angle, overall illumination of lower intensity. The quartz light (top right) is most popular, though it is often fitted with a fresnel lens (bottom right) to focus the beam or to soften the edges of a spot.

nation all over and no hint of the detail which gives it depth and helps it to come alive.

This means that while the key light has to be a hard light, the filler light must be softer. In other words, it must throw a more diffused beam which will provide a soft illumination to the shadowed side of the face, without casting more hard shadows of its own. Because natural light tends to cast shadows in one main direction, lighting your subject with two or more hard lights would produce a jumble of conflicting shadows which would create a confusing picture.

So, place your filler light — a soft photoflood, perhaps, for best results — on the opposite side of the camera from your key light. Then adjust its beam so as to lift the light level on the shadowed side of the face, so that you can see enough detail on the screened image. Once again, move the light backwards and forwards, and adjust its height up and down to produce the best combination.

Now you have two of your lights in place, look again at the picture on the screen and compare it with the view you have when looking directly at your subject. The biggest difference of which you should still be conscious will be in the relationship of the subject to the background. In reality, you can see the wall behind your subject's head well enough, in the light scattered from the rest of the room. On the screen, the background will either tend to vanish into darkness, in the contrast with the fully-lit face, or it may be partly illuminated by light thrown from the key and filler lights. Either way, it will present a distraction, one which can only be eliminated by adding some extra illumination to lift the background to the kind of level perceived by the eye.

This is done by the third light in the basic lighting kit: the 'back' light. Like the key light, this should be another hard light, but it should be angled to miss the subject altogether, apart from casting an extra sparkle on his or her hair to help them stand out from the background. But this effect should be left to the very edge of the area of light cast by the back light. The main target is the background itself. Too much light cast onto the subject would weaken this effect, and perhaps create more confusing shadows to spoil the effect already created around the subject's face. You can try different places for the back light, but you will probably find the best effects can be produced by having it on the same side of the subject as the key light, but slightly behind, rather than in front of, him or her.

The back light completes the basic lighting arrangement for a single subject, though it's clear that this is a complete simplification of the kind of lighting needed for most scenes. For example, if you were shooting an interview or conversation between two people, then in theory each one would need three lights to achieve this kind of properly-lit, three-dimensional effect. In these circumstances, you could light each shot separately, moving the lights whenever the conversation shifts from one to the other. This would produce ideal conditions, at the expense of losing all spontaneity from the interview and stretching out the time taken to shoot it to an impossible extent. Better to accept a compromise and light the scene as a whole, with one subject's key light arranged to scatter enough light on the other subject to act as a filler, and a single back light to cover the background to both. But each extra person, or each extra focus of interest, will add another requirement to the lighting setup — and that's without worrying about the effects of any of the people in the scene actually getting up and walking about!

TAILORING YOUR LIGHTING

Let's now look at the factors which have to be taken into account in lighting an indoor scene. In this case, the job is more complicated than the fairly simple task of creating an even background for the faces of your subjects. If you have a living room which you want to use as scenery for a conversation or an event, like a record of a family party, for example, then the effect you need to produce is the existing lighting present in the room, but intensified to the level where the video camera can do justice to the scene when it finally appears on your television screen.

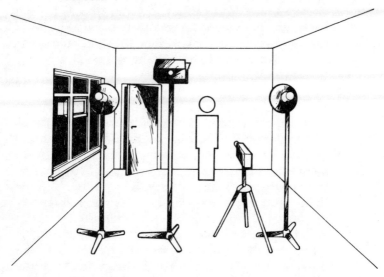

Figure 31. Lighting a wider area — for example, in a scene for a play or a group interview — calls for a more ambitious battery of lights to successfully cover the whole setting.

It's slightly easier if we look at creating an evening scene first, where all the lighting is artificial, and daylight doesn't need to be taken into account. Try looking at the scene through half-closed eyes, to see it as the camcorder will see it, or switch the camera on, and watch the result on the television screen to see *exactly* what the camera is recording. You will be most aware of the existing lights — a standard lamp behind the sofa perhaps, a wall light to the right of the door, or even a table lamp beside the fireplace. Next, look for the areas where the light cast from these different sources illuminates the floor, the furniture, or the walls. This is the picture you will have to create as accurately as possible, while lifting the light intensity to the point where the camcorder will see things as your eyes do when looking into the room.

Begin by trying to intensify your light sources. If the bulbs themselves can't be seen by the camera, because of the angles of the lampshades or the directional spotlights, then you can fit stronger bulbs to intensify the light they cast on their surroundings. Another way of increasing the light thrown on the floor and the walls is to use more lights, aimed at the right parts of the background, but hidden from the camera by being out of the shooting area or concealed behind the furniture.

You can make the most of the lights you have by using reflectors. We've seen how to use sheets of reflective material, like kitchen foil, when shooting out of doors in very bright sunlight, to reflect the sunshine onto the shadowed side of a face to act as a filler. And you can use the same approach indoors to throw soft pools of light onto walls or furniture or even ceilings, to create the right effect. Use the sheet of kitchen foil on a frame to reflect hard light from bulbs as a second-rank spotlight — or make another frame with crumpled foil attached to it to act as a floodlight, throwing a softer and more diffused reflection.

Another factor which needs considering is the kind of mood you want to establish. If the overall light level is still on the dark and subdued side, rather like a shot of someone staring into a glowing fire, lost in thought with only a few lights scattered in the background, then the mood the scene will create in the minds of the audience will tend to be subdued and reflective too. For a party, though, you'd expect a brighter scene altogether, to emphasise the gaiety and animation of the event, so you would need to take the extra trouble to make the picture as bright as possible with the resources you have available. In each case, you are making the lighting work for you, in creating the mood you want the scene to portray.

What happens, though, when you want to create an indoor scene in the daytime? You still need to lift the light level indoors to the point where the camera is able to make it look lifelike, but unless you're able to afford special daylight-type filming lights, you're going to have to create this effect with yellowish artificial light, which doesn't mix well with real daylight. How can we solve this problem without mixing colour temperatures?

There are two answers to this question, both of them involving making sure all the light is effectively at the same colour temperature. If you want to suggest broad daylight, aided by just a little artificial light in the corners of the room, then you can turn the yellowish cast of your artificial lights into a bluer daylight cast by screening them with blue filters. These are sheets of blue gel which can be hung in front of the lights, or which can be clipped to what's known in the trade as the 'barn doors' of video lights, using bulldog clips. The result will be a scene which looks as if it's lit predominantly by daylight, and you may need to heighten the intensity of the light streaming in through the window — to make up for lifting the light level *within* the room — by putting an extra light or two outside the window, pointing inwards. Since these too are likely to be yellowish in the light they throw, you'll need to screen them with sheets of blue gel, either individually or by spreading it over the whole windowpane.

If, on the other hand, you need to suggest morning or evening light, then the yellowish cast of your artificial light is less of a problem. You can leave your interior lights alone, but the real daylight coming in through the window may be more difficult to eliminate. So this time, you need a sheet of orange-yellow gel to fit over the windowpane, and then if you need to boost the light coming in from the window, you can still add a light or two without needing to correct their temperature any further.

It may sound a dauntingly complex business, but it's a vital part of every professional television production, and good lighting, carefully laid out, will make a spectacular difference to the pictures you can record at home, or at work. As you grow more ambitious, you may even find that you want to spend a little more money on more powerful lighting, as you can very rarely have *too* much lighting available for when you need it. For example, one drawback of the use of filters to even out the colour temperature in mixed-daylight/artificial-light combinations is that they work by subtracting some of the light your lamps are producing. So, as always, the need is likely to be for light, and more light, and yet more light.

On the other hand, lighting has to be planned and used with care. When shooting outside, you have light which tends to be even, except when you're placed in shadows cast by buildings or the land-scape. But when shooting indoors, you need to use the lighting as an extra ally to help make sure your audience's attention is focused fairly and squarely on what you want them to concentrate on. It's no good putting your subject — presenter, interviewee, or whatever — in subdued lighting next to a part of the scenery which is brilliantly illuminated, like a sofa or potted plant. If you do, they will focus immediately on the pot plant or the sofa, and when the subject moves or speaks, it will be a distraction instead of a clear and logical part of the action.

So this introduces yet another factor into your lighting plan. You have to light for mood, you have to light for effect, in making the scene look lifelike for morning, evening, twilight or midday, and you have to light to concentrate on the main areas of interest in each of your shots. Sometimes these may seem to be impossible objectives to reach in the same scene, but careful compromise will solve most problems. If the lighting plan works well, but your subjects are in the wrong place for the best effect, try moving them, or moving the furniture on which they sit, or through which they move. And move-ment is yet another potential problem which must be borne in mind.

Imagine you have a room, perfectly lit for where you want your subjects to sit — but you want one of them to enter through a door, walk into the room and sit down. You will need to check the effect of that movement on your scene. Can you see through the open door as your subject enters, to a dark hallway which seems pitch-black compared with your well-lit room? Then you will need a filler light in the hallway to make it look as if it's at least partially lit — or you need to move the camera slightly, or change the framing of the shot or the way your subject comes through the door, so that you *don't* see the hallway beyond. Now check the walk through the room —does the movement cast any confusing or unwanted shadows on the other people already present? If so, you may be able to solve the problem with an extra light or two (remember, you can *never* have too many lights), or by shooting the entrance into the room as two separate shots, or by changing the route of your subject's walk.

This may sound difficult, and no-one would pretend it's something which can be sorted out quickly or easily. It takes time, and practice, and experience. But if you approach lighting like someone learning a new language, which in a sense it is, you should have few problems. Take your time, proceed step by step from what you *can* do to what you *want* to be able to do, work within the limits of your equipment and your experience, and you may well be pleasantly surprised by the effects you are able to create. In fact, being able to build up scenes of progressively greater complexity through sensitive and careful lighting is one of the most vital parts of the challenge of professional production.

In time, when you feel happy enough with the rules of good lighting, you can begin to experiment with breaking those rules in the interests of creating particular effects for individual reasons. For example, the rule of not shooting a subject against the light is worth breaking if what you want is a dramatic silhouette — but avoid direct sunlight, or any source of light so powerful that it overwhelms your chosen subject. Better by far to choose a soft, diffused light source spread evenly over the background, such as a frosted glass window, or a window which is toned down by spreading a sheet of tracing paper over it to reduce the amount of light coming in.

Figure 32. Using light for dramatic effect — out of doors at a flying display, where the black silhouette of a low-flying aircraft shot against the bright sky adds extra drama, or indoors where a single light on one side of a subject's face leaves the other side in shadow in a deliberate 'chiaroscuro' effect.

You can also experiment with other variations on this theme. After all, a black silhouette is dramatic, but limited. Perhaps you want a little light and shade, to strive for a deliberate chiaroscuro effect. In that case, you shoot against the light, but lift the front of your subject's face with an additional light, effectively acting as a filler against the light flooding in from behind them. The result can be a very effective cameo portrait, ideal for heightening a particularly dramatic moment in whatever story you happen to be telling. It doesn't have to be a scripted drama, either — someone in the act of blowing out the candles on a birthday cake could be highlighted in this way as, for that particular moment, they are very much the centre of attention.

As far as the actual lighting you use is concerned, it's worth recalling that the best domestic lights to boost with more powerful bulbs are those which allow you to move, and rearrange the light as you want it. Spotlights on stands or overhead tracks, or swivelling desk lamps can make ideal impromptu video lights, but you have to be careful in two areas. Some lamps have a limit on the power of the bulbs you can use in them, because of the potential danger of overheating. In any case, it's a good idea to save power as much as possible by switching them off whenever you're not shooting.

The other point you need to remember is to keep the colour temperature as constant as you can. Shooting in a kitchen with overhead fluorescent lights will provide a bluer cast, closer to daylight than artificial light. Adding tungsten bulbs as spotlights will only produce patches of a yellower light, which will add to the complication of producing a set of lifelike pictures through the camera, particularly when the mixture of spotlights and overhead light may vary in individual close-up shots.

Perhaps the best compromise, to begin with, is to improvise two lights through fitting stronger bulbs to domestic spotlights or desk lights, and using a proper photoflood or, preferably, a video light with directional 'barn doors' and a control which allows you to vary the beam between a small spot of concentrated light and a wider flood of light, as your main light source. This gives you enough lights to light a single subject properly, and to show the principles of studio lighting which can be followed through, in time, to much more complex and ambitious subjects.

Finally, a word or two of warning. Lighting does use up a lot of power, and it does dissipate a lot of power in heat as well as illumination. So you always need to be careful about overloading domestic electrical circuits. Don't risk blowing fuses by running too many lights from one source, don't risk domestic light fittings overheating and even catching fire, and

128

don't leave lights on longer than necessary, especially if you have a whole battery of them illuminating a room. You also need to be especially careful when moving lights or camera. Switch the lights off, and place the lens cap over the camera, so that there's no likelihood of powerful beams entering the lens and causing internal damage.

You also need to watch out for unwanted reflections off mirrors, panes of glass or any bright objects in the room. One option is to move them out of the way — if they seem essential to the scene, then you can buy special sprays to dull the reflecting surfaces, so that they don't transmit light back into the camera lens as a distractingly bright spot in the middle of an otherwise subdued scene. Other options to kill unwanted reflections include covering the reflective surface with sticky tape, if the critical region is small enough, or spraying wider areas with a water mist to produce instant condensation so bright objects still look bright, without the reflections being troublesome in the overall scheme of things.

Figure 33. Different types of reflecting surface, like sheets of kitchen foil, or diffusers like silk screens or tracing paper (top row, left to right) can be used to tone down bright spots and reflect light into dark corners. Surfaces which reflect the lights too brightly, like glass or polished furniture can be toned down with matt spray, water mist or black tape (bottom row, left to right).

CHAPTER SEVEN

SOUND ADVICE

Video camcorder users have one enormous advantage over film camera operators — whenever they shoot anything, the sound is automatically recorded in synchronisation with the picture. Not only does this mean a separate sound recorder isn't needed, it also makes it possible to dispense with all the routine and paraphernalia required to match the sound to the picture at the editing stage by referring to a clapperboard or a microphone tap.

None of that is needed with a camcorder. In fact, since all home video cameras are equipped with microphones mounted on top of the camera body, it's quite difficult *not* to record sound when you're shooting pictures. You don't even have to think about it — up to a point. But the fact still remains that for the quality of the sound to match a well-constructed picture sequence, it's worth paying some extra thought to this often-neglected branch of video programme-making.

EXPLORING THE AUDIO OPTIONS

Let's begin by looking at microphones. The kind of microphone you'll find supplied as part of your camera kit is probably a compromise between highly directional microphones, like rifle mikes and the omni-directional mikes so often used for specific effects. These terms refer, not to the way a microphone works, nor even to its quality, but to the area from which it picks up its sound. High-quality rifle mikes can be made to pick up sound over a very narrow arc indeed — as the name implies, you almost have to aim them, like a rifle, at the subject whose sound you want to record. This can be useful where you want to concentrate on a particular sound, cutting out as much as possible of any other background sounds which might detract from your objective.

The omni-directional mike comes in when you have exactly the opposite objective. You want the complete sound picture from all points of the compass, without sounds from any one direction being

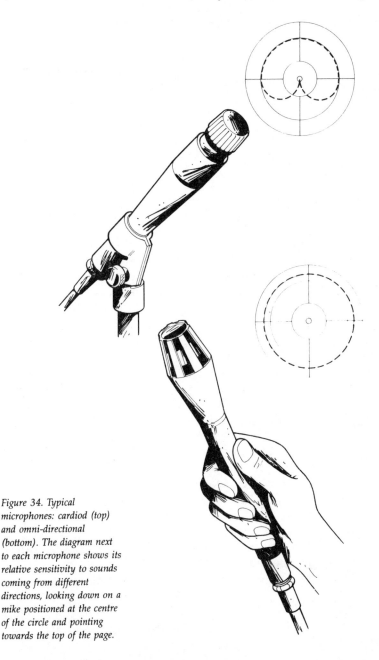

Figure 34. Typical microphones: cardiod (top) and omni-directional (bottom). The diagram next to each microphone shows its relative sensitivity to sounds coming from different directions, looking down on a mike positioned at the centre of the circle and pointing towards the top of the page.

particularly over-emphasised at the expense of the others. Where you need all-round atmosphere, rather than the sounds made by a particular subject, then this is the mike you need.

What you get, fastened to your camcorder, is usually a combination of the two. It will pick up sounds most clearly from the direction in which you're pointing the camera, but it will also pick up some of the background sounds from other directions too. This can be fine, when that kind of mixture of sound inputs is what you want — but you can achieve much more if the balance between subject sound and background sound were more under your own control.

Fortunately, microphones — even quite good-quality microphones — are a great deal cheaper than camcorders. This means you should invest in two, if you possibly can: a directional mike and an omni-directional mike, to give you the kind of selectivity your camera mike won't provide. Check that your camcorder has an external mike socket, and that the connections are compatible. In most cases connecting the other mike to the system automatically switches off the camera mike, so that your sound will still come from a single source.

There's another advantage to using separate micro-phones. In addition to being able to choose the sounds your camera will pick up, you can also connect them to the camera with extra-long leads, giving you another measure of selectivity. Instead of having to record all sounds from the camera position, you can move the microphone to the source of the sound you particularly want. This, in itself, has two advantages. You can pick out indivi-dual sounds, which allows you to make more of them, to create a dramatic effect. And, in recording an interview or a prepared piece being delivered to the camera, the closer your microphone is to your subject, the less it will be inclined to pick up other sounds. It can be quite surprising how noisy the world is, even in apparently tranquil locations:

traffic noise, aircraft high overhead, even birdsong, can be picked up all too well at times. This can partially blanket the words and, if it's a sound which isn't present all the time, can give the game away when you have to edit a contributor's response to a question. In the first part of his answer, you may hear a car or aeroplane in the background — then suddenly it disappears, revealing that the tape has been edited at that point.

One more point which you must bear in mind when using microphones. It's quite acceptable for someone to hold a microphone when they're delivering a piece to the camera, or when they're interviewing someone. But as a general rule, if you can conceal the microphone, it's better to do so. For interviews, you can buy small lapel mikes which appear rather like a small brooch or tiepin, especially if you conceal the cord under shirt or jacket. Or you can hold the mike on the end of a boom (fastening it to the end of a broom handle with a bandage of adhesive tape is an easy expedient) and use this to aim the microphone at the subject, from just out of shot. Whatever you do, don't let the mike or the mike cable appear in shot, unless it's being used by the presenter. That's on a par with getting the camera crew, the director or even the instruction manual into the shot, or having a contributor look at the camera and ask 'Do you want me to say my bit now?'. We all know these things happen, but keeping them out of the programme means taking that little extra trouble to produce professional results. So even if you need to place your mike on the far side of the scene to pick up the sound you want, camouflage it, and the cable, as thoroughly as you can.

MIXING SOUND SOURCES

There is still a serious limitation to the sound you can apply to your video programmes. On a professional production, the soundtrack you hear is a mixture of people speaking to camera, interviews, background sound, sometimes with special effects added to heighten a particular mood, and music. But many camcorders and VCRs limit you to a single sound channel. You can record actuality — the sound background at the time you shoot the pictures — on this channel using the microphone mounted on the camera with no problems at all. But if you subsequently record a commentary or some background music onto the programme, this will record over the existing sound, and obliterate it in the same way as recording a new picture sequence onto the tape would overlay and erase the existing material.

If you have a hi-fi stereo model with an audio-dub facility, you can record new sound on the mono edgetrack while retaining the original sound on the hi-fi tracks. Some camcorders, and VCRs, will allow you to play back a mix of the two, giving you the desired effect. If your camcorder does not offer audio dub (most Video 8 models don't) then one possibility would be to record your commentary as part of the shot. In the case of presenter sequences (which we'll come to later) and interviews, the words are the main part of the sound you'll be recording anyway. But trying to speak your own voice-over to shots, which you have to concentrate on in any case, is going to multiply your problems. The slightest slip over the words, and however perfect your pictures, you'd have to repeat the shot again. Better to add your commentary afterwards, as part of a properly mixed soundtrack, as the professionals do. By timing your commentary to the finished programme, you can say exactly what you want to say (see Chapter 11 on scripting a commentary), and you can suit the words to the pictures and to the timing of the programme, for the most professional result.

But how can you do that without obliterating the existing soundtrack? The answer is, you take a leaf from the professional's book, by taking the soundtrack from the camera tape and mixing it separately before copying it back onto the finished programme. And for that, you'll need some extra equipment. You can either use a pair of audio recorders to mix your different sound inputs — from the videotape material shot on location, from your voice-over commentary and from any additional sound effects or music tapes — onto a single channel, which you can then dub onto your edited programme tape at the edit stage. This is more or less what is done (on much more elaborate and expensive equipment) with broadcast television programmes, but for the home video-maker, it's a trifle laborious.

Happily, there is an alternative. Manufacturers are now becoming more aware of the high expectations of today's camcorder buyers, and are beginning to introduce more and more ambitious, semi-professional equipment to their ranges. One very valuable addition to any programme-maker's kit list is a stereo sound mixer. This allows you to simplify the mixing of two sound sources onto one channel — commentary and sound effects, commentary and music, or music and effects — of the edited programme.

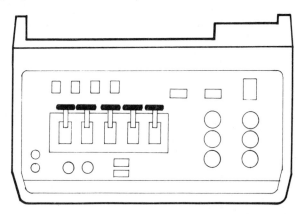

Figure 35. A typical sound mixer, with fader switches on the left-hand side for up to five inputs, and a series of meters on the right to show the level of each of the inputs, and the selected output being recorded on the tape.

Equipment like this, with separate audio and video faders, microphone connections and additional facilities like echo and other special effects, make the sound editing of your programme easier — at a price. The important point to remember is that it doesn't matter whether you opt for the cheaper and simpler pair of audio recorders and more laborious

135

method, or whether you buy a specialised audio mixer which does more of the work for you. The target in both cases is exactly the same; what you need to complete your programme and complement your pictures is a well-balanced combination of voices, sound effects and background music, properly blended so that no one element over-whelms the others, and synchronised to the edited pictures. If you can deliver that, by whichever method you choose, the result will have a genuine professional gloss, which is well worth the extra trouble taken to produce it.

CHAPTER EIGHT

GRAPHICS

Virtually every television programme you'll ever see uses graphics somewhere, if only for the opening and closing titles, to give you the name of the programme and the names of the people who helped to make it. But graphics appear in all kinds of other roles too — to identify people being interviewed, to reinforce facts and figures being quoted in the programme, to introduce different parts of the programme, to identify locations and to provide additional background information of every type. But where professional programme-makers can produce lettering quickly — using keyboard-type graphics generators which allow you to type in the lettering you want to see on the screen, and then to decide on its size and positioning — until recently home video producers have had nothing in the way of similar facilities to rely on.

GENERATING TITLES

But some of the latest breed of camcorders feature character generators as part of the package, or as an optional extra which can be bought separately. The optionals look like a television remote control, with a series of buttons to control different functions and to provide a complete alphanumeric (letters and figures) keyboard, and they are normally plugged into a dedicated socket located somewhere about the camera body.

The object is to be able to write any captions which you want to superimpose on whatever it is you're shooting —a very useful facility for naming individuals or locations, or creating opening and closing titles. With the more sophisticated generators, different buttons allow you to select capitals or lowercase letters, or to control the captions you write so they occupy different parts of the screen. You can produce a whole series of captions, as cards, and control when one is replaced by the next, the time clearly depending on how much information you've written on the screen in each case. Generally speaking, you need to allow the audience time to read each screen-load of information twice, fairly slowly, before switching to the next. And you can produce a long list of titles, which you can set to continue scrolling up the screen over whatever the camera is shooting at the time — an ideal way to produce professional end-credits and close your programme with a list of those who helped or contributed in any way.

But the usefulness of this extra facility does not stop there. If it was a case where you wanted to put over a particular piece of information as a graph, with a written title and a set of pictures, then because the character generator combines the letters you set with the picture being seen by the camera, you can create the graph in reality, and then add the title and the figures electronically. All you need to do is find a sheet of coloured paper, add a pair of axes and the line of the graph with coloured tape, in a contrasting colour, and the character generator can be used to do the rest.

Set the graph up on a backing card to hold it flat and mount the camcorder on the tripod plate. Point the camcorder squarely at the card — unless the axis of the lens is perpendicular to the paper, the horizontals and verticals on the paper (like the axes on the graph) won't look straight — and frame the graph carefully, leaving space for the characters you want to add. Then try adding the titles and the figures you want to incorporate into the graph, moving them where necessary, and reframing the picture where there isn't enough space for the letters you want to fit in. Since this, by nature, is a static shot, all the work that's required to bring it off is in the preparation. Once the diagram is finished to your satisfaction, you can then record it for as long as it should take the audience to absorb the information which it contains.

If you don't have this kind of facility on your camera, then that doesn't limit you to having to do without graphics altogether. Granted, you won't be able to superimpose lettering on pictures in quite the same way, but a little ingenuity can still enable you to produce some varied and sophisticated effects. All you need is a set of cards of the right size and colour, and you can either draw in your own lettering and symbols, or use sheets of dry-print letters like Letraset, which you simply rub off the backing paper and onto your card exactly where they're needed.

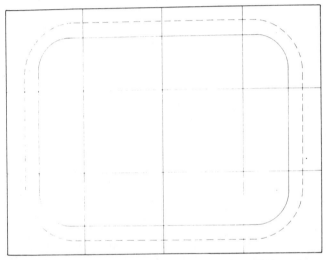

Figure 36. The rounded corners of the TV screen, together with the surface curvature, means that titles too close to the edge of the picture can't be read easily. Better to keep them within the safe area shown by the unbroken line.

Let's begin with the cards first. These need to be cut to the proportions of a television screen — three units deep and four across — and an ideal size would be about a foot across by about nine inches deep. Much smaller than that, and your lettering would have to be cramped — much larger and most of the standard sizes of Letraset would be too small to be read easily when played back on the screen. It's a good idea if the cards themselves are pale buff or grey, since these will appear almost white on the screen, but would be less likely to produce troublesome reflections than a pure white card might do. And an additional tip worth bearing in mind is to draw a light pencil line about an inch and a half in from the edges all the way around the card. The area of card within this line is called the 'safe area' and this is ideally where lettering and other graphics displays should be concentrated. Anything outside this line is in danger of vanishing into the curved edges of the television screen when the recorded tape is played back.

Figure 37. Simple titles either drawn by hand or using dry-print lettering. Keep lettering bold and simple, in either solid or outline characters.

What kind of letters should you use? Generally speaking, bold, simple typefaces work best, without fine lines or elaborate embellishments or serifs which the camcorder will tend to lose when the picture is recorded. Most dry-print lettering is either white or black. Using white lettering gives you the option of colouring it afterwards to produce the kind of effect you want. If you are adding extra colours to your lettering, it's better to use pale, pastel shades, since the camera is happier with these colours. Deep colours, like vivid reds, and harsh contrasts like blues and greens, don't seem to produce as pleasing an effect when seen through a video camera as quieter combinations do.

Once your titles have been prepared, you can shoot each card separately for the right amount of time for the message to be absorbed. Ideally, the cards should be fixed to a vertical surface, with the camera set on its tripod at a height equal to the mid-point of the card, and aimed and focused at this centre point.

This guarantees that the horizontals and verticals will be straight lines, though you will have to check that the top and bottom of the card is level. To light the card properly you need one light on either side of the camera, of approximately equal power, and angled at about forty-five degrees to the paper. To avoid any tendency towards awkward reflections, position the lights slightly above the camera angled slightly downwards towards the paper.

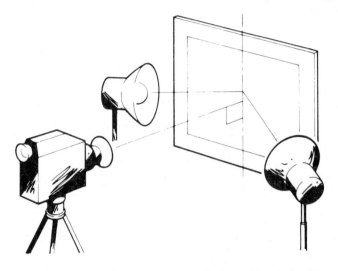

Figure 38. Shooting stills and title cards, with the card held vertically at the same level as the camera, and a pair of lights on either side of the camera.

As you continue to look through a succession of cards, it's a good idea if you make sure that the words on each are in approximately the same place. This means that as you record each card in turn, with a cut to the next one, and the next, and so on, the progression will be fairly smooth rather than a succession of jump-cuts. If you find you have a lot of titles to record, you could even mount the cards in a frame or in a ring binder, so that all you have to do between shots is lift the top card out or flip over a sheet in the ring binder, to cut the recording time down to a minimum.

You can even record a set of credit titles scrolling up the screen by using what television producers had to use before graphics generators were invented. You draw out the titles on a long sheet of paper which is stuck down on the edge of a large-diameter drum which is mounted on a horizontal pivot, so that it can be turned very slowly. You stand the camera edge on to the drum, and focus it on the nearest point of the drum's circumference. All you then have to do is switch the camera to record as you rotate the drum slowly, and the titles mounted on its edge will scroll slowly up the screen.

Another idea which can link the titles more closely to the programme itself is to take a series of pictures with a stills camera while you're out on location shooting the programme. If you have the best of these enlarged to the same size as the graphic cards, you can use them as backgrounds to the titles. You can either write the credits in white on sheets of transparent gel, which you can mount one after the other in front of the photograph for a title sequence with the same picture, you can even build up a graph by putting different parts of it on different sheets of gel, and adding them in succession to the background photograph, or you can use a series of pictures, one for each card of the titles, so that the picture changes every time the graphics change. In fact, you don't even need to take the pictures yourself. It's often possible to find pictures of the right kind of subject in the pages of glossy magazines or colour supplements which will do the job nearly as well.

One device which is often seen in television graphics is the title which is actually written on the screen as you watch. You can do this yourself by using a blackboard or a set of Letraset letters or even a set of children's lettered building blocks. Divide your title sequence up into a series of shots, each shot being as short as possible, and each time either add a single letter or even a short word, depending on the length of the shots and the overall speed at which you're aiming. If you can make these titles an integral part of your programme, so much the better. A title with building blocks would be perfect for a video of a child's birthday party; a title chalked on the wall would suit a documentary on a neighbourhood development scheme for example.

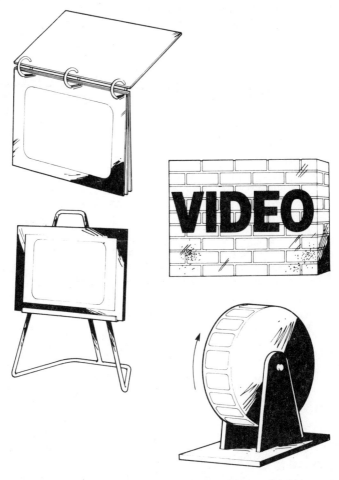

Figure 39. Different ways of producing professional titles — either by mounting them on a series of cards which can be flipped over quickly while shooting, or by drawing them on part of the subject being shot. Titles can also be mounted on an artist's easel, or on the edge of a large drum, which is turned slowly so the list of captions runs up or down the screen.

You can produce rather more ambitious graphics by using simple animation. If you build up a multi-layered title card, you can write some of the information on the top layer, then pull this top layer away (with your hands out of shot) to reveal another

143

layer of information, and then another, and so on. You can mix drawings and words, so that a drawing of a train pulls on the title of the railway programme, or a car pulls away from the kerb, leaving the title 'The Journey' written on the road surface. Either way the only limit is your own artistic ability, and your originality, because it's often possible to assemble these pictures from photographs, line engravings, posters or other existing picture sources. All you need is a multi-layer construction, and hand grips which allow you to pull away different parts of the diagram smoothly and unobtrusively, with your hands out of shot the whole time.

OTHER TITLING METHODS

More and more modern camcorders offer a clever little facility which makes it easier to produce top-quality graphics with a minimum of time and fuss. All you need is a card with either a title or caption written on it, and perhaps a set of basic shapes like a rectangle or a circle in a contrasting colour to the background. Controls on the camera not only allow you to record one or more of these images in the camera's memory, but you can also select the colours in which you want the captions to be shown on the screen, and also instruct the camera to superimpose the captions or the shapes on the pictures you are actually recording.

If you want to make a video of the family playing beach cricket, you can store a circle (representing a cricket ball) in the camera's memory, along with the title 'Seaside Test Match' on another frame in the memory (provided, of course, it can store two). Then when you start shooting the match in progress, you can set the camera controls to call up the frame with the 'Seaside Test Match' title and press another button at the time you want the title to appear superimposed on the picture you are recording. Press the same button again and the title disappears. You can then call up the frame with the circle on it, and start shooting from another angle. When you want to pause the action, or change to another part of the match, you press the titles button, and the picture is contained in a circle, until you cut to another picture and then remove the symbol. With the addition and removal of titles and graphics like this, and the use of still pictures and slides which can be recorded and worked into the action in a similar way, and the use of the fade controls, you have a useful battery of effects at your fingertips.

Finally, you can buy one of the new and still more ambitious graphics generators now available for the home video market. These offer the choice of several different fonts, or typefaces of lettering, together with useful symbols and outlines, and the opportunity to draw your own titles with a special pen on a graphics tablet. These effects, together with the facility for making the finished titles scroll up and down the screen, allow you to add titles to your programme at the editing stage which will match the standards of many professional productions.

But you don't have to resort to relatively expensive electronics to produce professional titles. If you can think of a way of making your titles part of what you shoot, you can produce some first-class effects. Even a video of a game of beach cricket on a summer holiday, provided you write the title in the sand before you start, and use the beach as a graphics drawing board for captions, score cards and other comments as the game progresses, can have a totally professional appearance. The steam-railway programme we used as our example earlier could have its titles written out using Letraset in the style of a railway timetable. Placed over a genuine timetable on the station noticeboard on the day of the shoot, held in place with Blu-Tack and shot with a few wisps of steam drifting past and all the background noise of engine whistles and station announcements, this would produce an effect which couldn't be bettered with all the technology in the world.

CHAPTER NINE

SPECIAL EFFECTS

Whenever we watch television, we can hardly help noticing the amazing variety of special effects which are brought to bear on everything from children's serials to promotional trailers. Some are picture effects — the picture you've been watching is rolled over, or flipped, or shrunk or flattened or distorted into all kinds of different shapes. Images can appear as part of other images, people can be made to appear as if they're part of a scene thousands of miles away — or they can be made to change, talk to an identical self on the other side of the room, or disappear entirely. New pictures can be made to appear from nowhere — or from parts of the furniture, or mirrors on the wall, or from the tiniest and most insignificant detail in the previous scene. Or, through the immensely powerful computer-graphics systems, they can be created entirely from the imagination of an artist, working throughout from electronics.

There's another kind of special effects too, which is common to both television and feature films in the cinema. This is not so much involved with creating a new reality by electronic means, but by producing a convincing illusion of reality in optical terms. In other words, producing a severed limb for a horror movie, or a spaceship docking at a space station for a science fiction sequence, or a convincing explosion for a cops-and-robbers series — even when they're done with stuntmen, models, or controlled explosives and smoke bombs, or by clever make-up and fake blood (called 'Kensington Gore'), they all count as special effects. In some cases, such as the 'Star Wars' series, the money spent on the ambitious special effects accounted for a large part of the budget — and rightly so, since the results accounted for a major part of the films' appeal.

Unfortunately, this is one area where the amateur programme-maker's resources are bound to be severely limited. Even simple dissolving from one image to another — a 'mix' — is well beyond the present state-of-the-art video equipment, and it's likely to remain one area where video shooting lags behind cine home-movies for some time to come. A simple dissolve on a movie camera can be done by a carefully pre-planned double exposure, but there's no practical way of doing that inside the most expensive of video cameras.

MIRROR MAGIC

But there are one or two useful tricks which can be made to work quite well, with a little ingenuity and pre-planning. A simple 'wipe' effect is a neat alternative to a mix, where instead of one picture dissolving into another, the new image simply wipes across the screen, blocking out the old one as it moves. This can be done with a large, good-quality mirror, provided the two scenes you want to use in your wipe effect are close enough together for the mirror trick to work.

Let's assume that you want to wipe from a distant background in one direction, to someone delivering a piece to camera against a different part of that background. You set up your camera with the mirror angled in front of it so that, when looking through the viewfinder, all you see is the background reflected in the mirror, looking like a direct view of the scene itself — except that you will have to choose a shot where the left-right reversal produced by the mirror won't be obvious to the audience.

Then you move the mirror out of the way, leaving the camera locked in position on its tripod, and you pose the presenter in the right spot for the framing to be correct (remember, you can't move the camcorder) and far enough away for there to be no need to change the focus. Put the mirror back, adjusting the angle so that the framing of the reflected shot is as you want it, set the camera into the pause mode, then as you press the 'start' button, give the signal for the mirror to be slid sideways, slowly and smoothly and without changing the angle with the subject. As soon as your presenter sees the mirror clear the camera lens, he or she knows they're in shot, and they can start saying their piece. The most difficult part is getting the mirror movement right, so that shakiness or a change in the angle between mirror and camera doesn't give the game away — and some kind of mounting, where the mirror slides in a channelled piece of wood to act as a support might help here — but when done properly, it can be a surprisingly effective shot. And your audience can't help wondering how you achieved it.

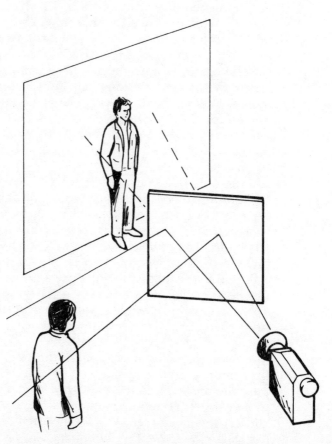

Figure 40. Using a mirror in front of the camera, carefully angled to provide a 'wipe' effect between (in this case) one presenter and another, set against different backgrounds.

Another special effect can be achieved with mirrors, but is really limited for title shots or more artistic or adventurous subjects. You need a set of three or four rectangular mirrors of identical size, which you can assemble into a tube of triangular section (rather like a Toblerone chocolate pack) or of square section, which you place over the camera lens, so that it's looking down the tube from one end to the other. Shoot the subject through that and, depending on the size of the mirrors and the way you've framed the shot, you should end up with some interesting kaleidoscopic effects, particularly with very colourful or very active subjects.

ANIMATION ANTICS

You can also experiment with a form of animation. If you fit the camera on a tripod and tighten up all the adjustments, it should stay perfectly fixed relative to the landscape. If you then record a few frames at a time — down to a fraction of a second or so per shot if your camera has a time-lapse record facility which will allow this — you can magnify any natural or deliberate changes in the landscape by spacing your recordings accordingly. You can see the tide come in to cover a beach in a few seconds, a car park fill and empty in about the same time, weather change from sun to rain, or sunshine deepen into twilight or darkness. All these things can be made to serve a purpose in telling a story, as well as being clever and intriguing shots in their own right. They can be used to suggest the passing of time or a change of mood — particularly in the case of the weather shot — or even, with a careful choice of subject, something more challenging, sinister, or funny.

This kind of time-lapse shot can also be made to work as an integral part of the action, by setting up your own action to treat in this way. The loading of an enormous amount of luggage into the boot of a car, the painting of a wall, the tidying up of a room — all can be made to happen by magic by concentrating on the changes and omitting any human figures altogether. You could try adding a person or two as an

Figure 41. A simple animation, with a single movement broken up into successive stages, and edited onto the tape to produce a smooth sequence — great fun to experiment with, and surprisingly effective.

experiment — ask them to freeze their positions whenever you record that fraction of a second for each shot, but between shots they can and should move as much as they like.

Some cameras have a supplied or optional remote-control unit which can help to make these animated sequences a lot easier. If the camera is securely mounted on a tripod and set up with the focus and framing correct, you can record a series of half-second shots of the surroundings using a special 'animation' button, and then press the start/stop button on the remote control unit every time you want to record one of these 'snapshots'. Once you have reached the end of the animated sequence, all you need do is press the 'animation' button again, and the camera reverts to normal operation.

You can even extend this kind of effect into more conventional animation, using plasticine figures whose shape can be changed shot by shot, or even children's toys whose arms and legs can be bent into position. Your only limitation is the time you have available, your own ingenuity, and the shortest shot your camera will allow you to record, even by overlapping one shot with the next to cut down the length of shots still further. But there is a way of being able to use this effect and several others: buying or borrowing a small movie camera, shooting a scene on film, and then copying the result onto tape. Because film cameras can be made to shoot frame by frame, smooth animation is much easier — and you can even shoot dissolves between different scenes, and slow-motion subjects too.

To make use of these effects in your video production, you need to re-record the processed film sequences on your video camera, at the right place in the programme. This means using a dedicated telecine transfer unit or a projector — preferably one with the facility to play back at 16⅔ or 25 frames per second (⅓ or ½ of the television and video rate) rather than the more common 18 and 24 frames per second used for film work. As you're going to have to edit each extract onto your programme tape as another shot, you'll need to make sure everything is running properly, and that both projector and camera are correctly focused, before you start recording. To reduce distortion to the minimum, stand the camera and the projector side by side, with the screen onto which you're projecting the film set at right angles to both of them. Adjust the framing, with the projector running, so that you capture most of the picture in the video viewfinder, though you're bound to lose a little of it because film cameras have a differently-shaped frame.

It's also helpful to have some kind of warning of the start of the sequence you want to record. It's easy enough to splice any film sequence in front of your special-effects shot to act as a leader — either a blank film with the countdown in seconds to the start of your own piece of film, or another shot with a clearly identifiable end to it, as a warning that your shot is about to follow it at the vital instant. A shot of someone diving into a swimming pool would be ideal, with the cut to your recording made at the moment they hit the water, giving you an unmistakable cue to press the 'start' button.

FROM SCI-FI TO SIMULATED SOUND

There are more elaborate setups you can use to create an illusion of reality — many of them easier than you might think. For example, the deep space sequences showing enormously complicated space vehicles manoeuvring against a starlit background, and hanging without any visible means of support, are simple to stage. You need some convincing models, made from modified plastic kits and all kinds of oddments from margarine containers to press studs, painted in the right kind of colours and with a mass of small and complex detail to hint at a large construction a long way away. These are supported on stands which are painted matt black, so that they don't reflect the light, and they're arranged in front of a black background sheet, pierced with a pattern of holes to suggest a vast starscape from lights hidden behind the sheet. The lighting on the model has to be done carefully, so that it's quite subdued and casts deep shadows, as it would from a single star or planet close enough to illuminate the scene — a single light should do the trick, but angle it so that it doesn't show up the stand.

We've concentrated so far on visual special effects — but any scene can be made much more convincing with the right kind of soundtrack. But if the right effect isn't readily available, you can do an awful lot by playing tricks on your microphone, and making a sound which is close enough to the original to fool your audience. How many people know you can make the rubbing together of two sandpaper blocks sound like the approach of a steam train? Or that squashing a half-empty bag of flour with the right rhythm sounds like footsteps in deep snow? Or that you can use a vacuum cleaner to simulate the subdued whistle of jet engines?

Weather sound effects are always useful. Falling rain can be concocted by placing your microphone underneath a paper chute which then has castor sugar trickled down it steadily. Your story calls for heavier rain — a tropical downpour, perhaps? Hold a large sieve over your microphone, drop a couple of dozen dried peas into the sieve and roll them backwards and forwards. Wind? Draw a piece of silk across a wooden grating. Rustling of the trees? Rattle a handful of magnetic tape in front of the microphone. These are just a few of the tricks you can try. Like all special effects, they depend on ingenuity and invention, and hopefully these few examples will have whetted your appetite to try other ways to create the effects you want for your own programmes.

Here too, newly available technology is widening the choice available to the home programme-maker. Effects generators now on the market allow you to mix between two different pictures (two VCRs or a VCR and a camcorder), provided you have another VCR on which to record the output. In addition to mixes as such (remember, where one picture dissolves into another) they also allow you to carry out a whole series of wipes — the new picture comes in at one or more points on the screen and extends to cover the whole in a wiping action. Effects like these, or the keyed backgrounds which allow you to shoot a presenter in a studio, and superimpose a background suggesting he's out on location, are really more useful at the edit stage, which we'll come to later in the book.

CHAPTER TEN

IN FRONT OF THE LENS — PRESENTERS AND INTERVIEWS

All we've covered so far has related to producing a programme from behind the camera: deciding on a subject, researching, carrying out a recce, producing a treatment and shooting and recording the material, not to mention planning and understanding graphics and special effects. Now we're going to take a couple of steps forward, into the role of the on-screen presenter, because the best way you can learn how to get the most out of someone presenting your programme, is to try out the role for yourself.

DO-IT-YOURSELF PRESENTING

The first thing to understand about working in front of the camera is that there's no mystique about it. All kinds of people find they have a natural gift for communication through the television screen and even those who don't possess this inborn ability can still learn how to appear relaxed and convincing on screen. Many companies exist purely to train actors, politicians, and company executives in how to 'come over' well on television, so highly prized is this skill of talking to the camera. And in taking your first steps as an on-screen performer, you can arrange things so that you can try out your first practice sessions with no-one else watching. Not for you the intimidating presence of a full television crew, the lights, and the complex signals between the director and floor manager. You can practise in your own time, and in complete privacy, and you may well end up being surprised by how easy it is.

Let's begin by deciding where to practise talking to the camera. You've two main alternatives: indoors or outdoors. The advantage of indoors is that you have no travelling to do. You can set up a 'news studio' type background at home with a desk and a couple of lights, and you can work in complete privacy. The disadvantages are that unless you're careful with the lights, you may be so taken aback by the way your face appears in close-up, with shadows emphasised more than they would be with a more careful lighting combination, that you won't assess your performance with the objectivity it deserves.

An outdoor location in broad daylight avoids this problem. Another advantage is that if the background is unusual or unexpected it can provide you with a natural subject for conversation with the camera — but more of that in a moment. Do you need an assistant, to operate the camera? It makes life easier, in the sense that you have less to concentrate on, but if you feel happiest taking the first lesson on your own, there's no reason why you shouldn't mount the camera on a tripod and do the entire job yourself.

Let's assume that the first practice session is a solo one. Find yourself a location where you won't be disturbed, where the view provides a suitable backdrop to whatever you're going to say, and where there won't be problems of noise, or traffic or anything else to act as a distraction. First of all, decide where you're going to stand to deliver your piece to the camera — not with the sun behind you, or you'll disappear into a dramatic silhouette outlined against the glare. Mark the spot with an empty tape box, then move back to the camera and set up the shot as if you were shooting an imaginary person on that spot —which in a sense you are. It's a good idea to begin with an empty tape, since these first trials will be untidy and a certain amount of waste is inevitable.

Set the camera to begin recording, and walk back to your mark and look into the camera lens, counting

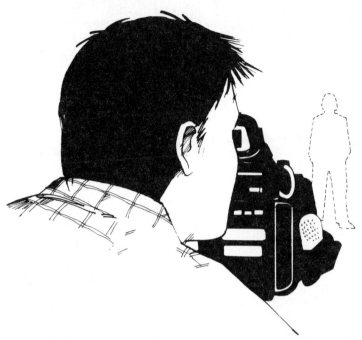

Figure 42. Setting the camera up, on its tripod, to shoot the marked position where you can stand and deliver your first trial speeches to camera.

from one to ten slowly. Then walk back to the camera, wind the tape back to the beginning, and replay what you've just recorded. What we are looking for now is your positioning — nothing more. Are you in the centre of the screen? Does the camera need to be tilted down or up to produce the shot you need — do you need to zoom in or out, or do you, as presenter, need to move your position to left or right? Make whatever corrections you think are needed, set the camera to record again, walk back to your mark, look into the lens, and count to ten all over again. Then walk back, rewind the tape, and check the results. Keep on doing this until you're satisfied that the shot, and your positioning, are right.

Of course, if you have someone who can help you, capable of lining up the camera to your instructions, then you can save a lot of time. Ideally, if your helper is another would-be video producer, then you can take it in turns to practise in front of the camera, and to operate the equipment so as to produce the best from your presenter. We'll come to all that a little later: for the time being, the real obstacle is learning how to talk to the camera.

For many people, this is the most difficult part to master. From childhood, we have been conditioned to think there is something slightly ridiculous about someone talking to himself or herself out loud, and someone speaking to an inanimate camcorder on a tripod can seem the next best thing. But you do have one advantage in this early practice session: apart from whoever you may have to help you, no-one else will be aware of what you're trying to do. If you've chosen your setting carefully, that is. You won't have the often intimidating background of a full television crew, all concentrating on every word of your delivery, and all in vain if you should forget your lines or stumble over a word, or move slightly out of frame.

The best way to approach the task is to imagine you're telling a story to an old and familiar friend. You need to speak clearly, you need to use words and phrases which make your story come alive in the telling, and you need to look at your friend — the camera — while you're relating the story. And that's really all there is to it. Except that you do need to make your delivery more fluid and lucid than would be the case in everyday conversation. Try to avoid any pauses, when at a temporary loss for words. Try not to ramble, and have to backtrack to pick up the thread of the story. And try not to stumble, or mispronounce words through changing your mind over what you intend to say.

But remember, always, that all these objectives relate to a smooth and polished and, above all, professional performance. No-one will expect you to hit the target first time — indeed, no-one will see whether or not you hit it, unless you show them the tape afterwards. And your helper will have the same problems getting his or her delivery right, so think positively and concentrate on finding something interesting to say; something about which you know a good deal, and something which you can talk about without having to search too diligently in your memory. That, at least, will give you one less factor to worry about.

Some people think the right way to speak to a camera is like the right way they would approach making a speech. They would spend a lot of time writing it, polishing it and improving it until it was just about perfect, and then they'd commit it to memory, learning it until they could reproduce it effortlessly from beginning to end. But there are two drawbacks to this approach. One is that it takes far too long, and more importantly, it will come over very badly indeed. You may remember all the words from start to finish, but unless you're a talented actor to begin with, they won't sound either sincere or spontaneous: we make up ordinary conversations as we go along, and this is the effect to strive for.

A prepared speech sounds contrived and stilted by comparison, even if you don't dry up halfway. When repeating something parrot-fashion, even when it's something you've written yourself, the danger is that your attention can wander. You can suddenly start thinking about the situation you're in, and then your memory can start playing tricks — without thinking about your words and what you want to say, you forget. You can't remember what comes next, and without a prompter, you're lost. So leave learning one's lines to the actors; that's what they're trained to do. A good actor can read a page from the telephone directory and make it sound interesting — but most of us can only do that with material *we* find interesting. Which means something new, something fresh, and above all something *we* feel strongly about.

You could try bringing along a book, or better still a newspaper, and use that — not as a script, but as a background briefing. Choose a section of the story, or a short news item, and read it through to yourself several times first. Don't make any attempt to learn it by heart though, for fear of falling into the recitation trap. Just memorise the details — any names, dates, places, figures, for example — and then try telling the story to camera. Don't worry if you dry up, or stumble over the words. Pause, looking straight at the camera (this gives you the chance to edit a cutaway in at that point, or switch to another take) and carry on. Then stop recording and play back the sequence.

Whatever you feel about the results — and in most cases it's likely to be a mixture of disappointment at the things which went wrong, and pride at the parts which really weren't so bad for a first attempt — build on that performance by looking through the piece one more time and trying again. In fact, try several times, and then move on to another part of the book or another story from a different page of the paper.

As you become more relaxed with the camera, try reacting to the subject matter. If the subject is an amusing one, try a smile. If it's an amazing or unlikely one, try thinking yourself into the kind of expressions and gestures you would use in telling this to a friend — perhaps reading them a piece aloud from a newspaper in the pub, in the train, or in the living room at home. In time, you'll find your performance is less wooden, more relaxed, more human, and more convincing.

Now let's try a completely unrehearsed talk to the camera. Try to think of a subject about which you feel very strongly; either something which you're very fond of, or probably better, some news item or some trend or some aspect of human behaviour which makes you very worried or very angry. Think for a moment or two — no more, as too much thought can be inhibiting since it gives you too much which you feel you *have* to remember — and launch into your piece. Don't worry about having to pause now and again. If your piece is genuinely spontaneous, which this is, then these pauses will emphasise that you're thinking for yourself, and not working from a script. Try the same technique with different subjects. Talk about a family occasion, or what happened at work yesterday, or a film, or a television programme you've seen recently. Anything, in fact, which doesn't mean you making something up in advance — any subject which will allow you to talk off the cuff, without having a prepared script, or without having to search around for what to say next.

When you've recorded half a dozen or more sequences, try playing the whole lot back at one sitting. You should find an obvious improvement in your relaxation and confidence in front of the camera — and with that knowledge, you should find it a much less daunting prospect than it was before. Carry on practising, with different subjects and, if time allows, at different locations, and you will find your performance continues to improve. Which brings with it two very important advantages: you are building the ability to present your own programmes where necessary, without letting down the pictures with faults in your own on-screen performance, and you're also understanding more about how to work with professional and semi-professional presenters, where these are needed for particular projects.

PRESENTING A PRESENTER

Now, let's turn to putting all this effort into context. Whoever the presenter may be — yourself, a friend, or someone brought in for the particular programme on which you're working — how should he or she be used to best advantage? There are two overriding reasons for using an on-screen presenter rather than limiting yourself to an off-screen voice-over. The first one is that a presenter in vision lends more interest to a part of the subject where little is happening, or where the material being described isn't particularly visual. Secondly, a presenter is seen by the audience very much as the man or woman on the spot. The very fact that they can be seen *there*, where the action they are talking about is taking place (or has very recently taken place) lends them an extra authority. Because they're where the action is, they must know what they're talking about, mustn't they?

This is why a professional delivery is so important. If the presenter looks tense, or nervous, or unsure of what they should say, that authority is soon dissipated, and they become the person on the spot who all too clearly *doesn't* know what's going on. If they have to refer to notes, and then read the material to camera, this too adds to the impression of uncertainty — with one all-important exception. If what they're reading is from a clearly identifiable specialist source — a book, a report, a summary of a court's proceedings, for example, which they couldn't be expected to have written for themselves — then the act of looking up the information and reading it to camera actually *reinforces* their authority instead of diluting it. So how can we be sure that our presenter, given the problems, provides the most convincing delivery?

The first requirement is to make sure you are using the presenter, whatever his or her experience or ability, where an on-screen presence actually adds something to your programme. As we said earlier, a presenter is most valuable for injecting a more personal voice into the programme, and for explaining and emphasising those parts of the script which may otherwise be difficult to cover with appropriate pictures.

For example, in covering a current issue of some kind, like a controversial road scheme or a public enquiry, a presenter can bring us up to date on what's happened so far; providing an historical perspective which may be difficult to create in any other way. And we've all seen television programmes where companies and institutions have refused to comment on what's been said. A good way to tell the audience about that refusal is to stand a presenter outside the headquarters of the body involved and explain what they were asked to do, and relate the words in which they announced their refusal.

There are probably hundreds of other ways in which a presenter can be used to make a subject more immediate and more intelligible to the audience. Presenters are useful for making explanations comprehensible. They can use gestures, or even simple props, to explain the principles behind something which may otherwise be very difficult to deduce from the pictures. A good presenter can interview contributors and generally anchor the programme together — and when you have a positive point or opinion to put over, seeing a presenter deliver it can be more convincing than the same words delivered by a disembodied voice-over.

But how can we use a presenter visually? A series of cuts to and from a subject to a presenter, then back to the subject, back to the presenter and so on, would be counter-productive — apart from being boring — as they would hint at a separation between subject and presenter which would work against the impression you're trying to create.

So try to think of ways in which you can make the presenter part of the action. Always try to compose the picture with the presenter in front of a background which is very much part of the subject you're covering. If you're making a programme on a race meeting, either place your presenter in the paddock, or in the stand, or in the car park, or even in the road outside, as long as what appears behind him or her in the picture says 'race meeting'. And experiment with pans to and from your presenter, with change-focus shots moving directly from subject to presenter and vice-versa (where the geometry of the subject and the surroundings allow), and even with having your presenter walk out from the subject-matter itself.

If you're shooting a boat, having the presenter climb out of a hatchway and walk to the edge of the deck, before delivering his or her piece to camera, would be an effective entrance to make. To return to our railway example in an earlier chapter, the presenter could make a piece to camera by appearing at a corridor window of the leading coach when the train is about to leave. By cutting from the end of the presenter's piece to a shot of the guard blowing his whistle, and then a shot of the train pulling out, you have a very powerful exit sequence to round off the story perfectly.

You can also bring in a presenter sequence a little more subtly than simply cutting to him or her from the previous shot — one example is the 'pan-to-presenter'. The shot opens with the camera looking at a scene appropriate to the story. After a second or two, to establish the shot, the camera pans to left or right where we see the presenter, against another part of the same background, delivering the piece to camera. You can synchronise the presenter's voice in two ways. You can give the signal for the piece to start, as the camera begins its pan, so the audience hears the presenter's voice and is prepared to see him or her in person.

There is another alternative, which you can use when the script calls for a slight pause, and when

Figure 43. Introducing a presenter on location, by panning from the opening frame (left) to reveal the presenter (right). You have the choice of hearing the presenter's first words over the opening picture, or when you see him in the frame — see which seems most natural.

164

there's enough significance in the background for the presenter to react to it. You start the pan, and this time reveal the presenter standing looking at the same subject as we, the audience, are studying in the frame. When the camera finishes moving, the presenter turns to face the camera and begins the delivery. In both cases the timing is crucial — in the first example, the presenter can easily be given the cue by the camera operator, since at that stage he is safely out of frame. The second case is more difficult, since at the time the delivery is due to begin, the presenter is in shot, but turned away from the camera. In that case, you need someone out of frame but within the presenter's arc of vision to pass on the camera operator's waved signal that it's time to turn to camera and begin the delivery.

You can produce a similar transition by starting the shot in close-up on a distant part of the scene, and then zooming back to find the presenter. Since the presenter can't tell what the camera operator can see in the frame, once again a cue needs to be given that it's time to start the delivery. And a third way of making the transition is to focus in close-up on an object in the foreground. By changing focus, the presenter is revealed in the background, and once again needs a wave to cue his delivery.

What about microphones? The most important decision is whether your presenter should carry a microphone as a badge of office as well as an aid to recording the sound — or whether a more subtle tie or lapel microphone will do the job just as well without destroying the apparent spontaneity of the conversation between presenter and audience. The important rule is, if you're using a hand-held microphone, then it needs to be fairly obvious. If you're using one of the tie or lapel mikes, then make sure that the cables and other connections are kept as unobtrusive as possible.

What will happen if your presenter has difficulty delivering the lines? One option is to discuss shortening and simplifying what you're asking them to say — if a piece is too long for them to deliver without drying up, then it may well be too long anyway. On the other hand, if the script demands a long and complex explanation, and there are no pictures to allow you to cut from the presenter in vision to a voice-over of the second part of the piece, then you are left with two alternatives.

The first is to bring in a means of prompting the presenter; to aid the memory in recalling words which will, in most cases, have been written by someone else. The method most commonly used in professional television is the autocue; a printed script which is scrolled upwards over a special screen reflected in a pane of glass held at an angle to the camera lens. The camera sees the presenter clearly through the glass — but the presenter sees the reflection of the script, and can read it directly while looking straight into the lens.

The other method, which some — but by no means all — presenters are able to use is to record themselves delivering the piece onto a miniature audio recorder, like a Walkman. They then place the recorder in a pocket, and play back the recording into a small earpiece which can't be seen by the camera. When they deliver their piece to the camera, they're repeating what their own recorded voice is saying into their ear, but a fraction of a second later. It takes an accurate sense of timing and a lot of concentration, but anyone who can master the technique can find it a powerful aid to delivering a long and complicated piece of script. But like anything else which isn't being said in your own words, and from your own thoughts, it does demand the extra skill of injecting the right amount of emphasis and animation to make it sound spontaneous and convincing.

You can try and achieve a similar result by using so-called 'idiot cards' — large pieces of card which are either fixed to the tripod (so the presenter can read them while still looking into the lens) or held up as close as possible to the camera. Don't try to write out the whole piece in this way. Discuss with the presenter which individual words and phrases would be most effective in steering them through the piece, and limit yourself to those, written boldly enough for the presenter to see them without squinting or peering at the cards. If you can't get all the material onto one card, you can use two, three or more. But the person holding them is going to have to get the timing right, so the presenter isn't pausing for the next card to come up before launching back into the delivery.

Figure 44. Prompting the presenter, with 'prompt cards' or 'idiot cards' — with key points written in large characters — held as close to the camera as possible.

The alternative to prompting the presenter is to break the piece up into two or more sections. Select a natural break in the script; the end of a paragraph, or at least a sentence break. Shoot the opening part of the sequence as originally planned, with the presenter in either long or medium-shot framing, until the break point has been safely passed. Then pause, zoom in to pick up the presenter in close-up and cue the delivery again, this time from just before the break point. If your presenter can cope with the second part of the delivery in one piece, then all you have to do is cut to the tighter framing at or about the natural break point. And, because the two versions have a degree of overlap at that point, the edit should be an easy one to time properly. But as with all cuts of this nature, make sure that continuity is as accurate as you can make it — the presenter's stance, gestures, expression, and as far as possible the background, must be consistent between the two versions.

If you need to add another break to make the piece manageable, it's always possible to reverse the previous cut and go back to a wide framing for the close of the piece. In fact, one desperate remedy is to pull back so wide that you can't actually watch the lip movements of the presenter, so that if all else fails, he can read the rest of the piece off camera, and you can edit it on afterwards!

But a better alternative, and one which makes more positive use of the presenter as an individual, is to keep close in for the third section of script and move to a different angle. Start the shot with the presenter still looking in the direction of the original camera position. When the shot has become established — allow a second or so — cue the presenter to turn and face the camera and deliver the final section of the piece. (Remember you will need someone out of camera range and within the presenter's field of view to give the cue on your instructions.) If this final section of the script calls for a special emphasis, this turn-and-resume technique can be very powerful.

PLANNING AND SHOOTING INTERVIEWS

Now we'll move to the other way of involving people in the programme: interviewing, and recording quotes from contributors. Many of the requirements are the same for interviewees as they are for presenters. Their words need to sound genuinely their own, and the more spontaneous and convincing their delivery the better. But there are two significant differences. They're being prompted, to an important extent, by the presenter or interviewer asking them questions, and reacting to their answers, which does help keep things moving. And today's television style means that they aren't usually looking and speaking directly into the camera lens, but looking off-camera in the direction of the interviewer. Even if we never see or hear a question being asked, the quote or statement from the contributor will still be delivered as if he's speaking to someone present with the camera, rather than to the camera itself.

This last point makes things easier, for two reasons. It's a great deal more natural, and less intimidating, to speak to a person than directly to a camera lens. Secondly, because the contributor's eyes are looking out of frame, it's much easier to use the prompt cards to reinforce his or her memory (when these are necessary) without this being obvious to the audience. But, as was the case with the presenter, make sure what's written on the cards is limited to the bare essentials — figures, dates, percentages, proper names, unfamiliar words, or any other important details.

Whatever you do, don't let anyone talk you into allowing them a full script of what they're going to say. Unless they're experienced actors, in which case they shouldn't need this kind of prop anyway, they will *sound* as if they're reading a prepared statement, and all the pace and spontaneity of the interview will be lost. If they are prone to panic, and tend to dry up after a fairly short interval, then take the interview question by question. Make sure that they know that, if they find themselves short of anything to say, they should simply freeze, looking straight at the interviewer, as this maximises the possibility of editing the next question and answer on after the pause.

Another possibility is to avoid the formal interview setup and just shoot the interviewee's individual answers in close-up, one by one. In the edited version of the programme, the interviewer's questions can be added in voice-over, but remember this technique is limited to two or three questions at best, and even then you need footage to bridge the gap when the questions are being asked.

Now to shooting an interview itself. Let's assume that you've decided, in planning what a particular contributor has to say, on a list of four questions which the presenter should put to him. Assuming that the interview will start with an introductory piece by the presenter, followed by a turn to the contributor, or even a straight cut to the two of them for the first time, the initial shot would show both the interviewer and the person being interviewed. But once the contributor starts answering the question, you can start zooming in to hold them in close-up for most of the answer. If it's simply a quote, rather than a formal interview, then the recording will start with their answer, framed in close-up anyway.

If the contributor and the interviewer are happy to continue, stay in close-up for the whole of the answer to the question. In fact, a professional crew shooting an interview would probably shoot the whole interview, however many questions were involved, as a close-up on the contributor. Then they would change the camera position to shoot each of the interviewer's questions in close-up, so that these could be edited into the finished sequence at the appropriate times. This means setting up the camera so that the questioner is looking past it in the opposite direction to the contributor. For example, if the contributor is slightly to the right of the screen, looking towards the left-hand edge of the screen (to give him 'talking room') then you need to pose the questioner on the left-hand side of the screen, looking to the right of the camera, for the geometry of the shot to work.

Figure 45. When shooting an interview, concentrate first on the answers (top picture). Once those have been recorded, you can shoot the questions and 'noddies' (lower picture) to be edited into the sequence later.

Because these reaction shots tend to involve a nod of the head, they're known in television as 'noddies', and they're usually shot once the interview is over. But they serve an important purpose. If an answer to a question has to be shot in several sections, a cut to one of the questioner's 'noddies' provides an instant cutaway to bridge the jump-cuts which would result from editing the different pieces of the answer together.

What are the priorities from the interviewer's point of view? Ideally, he or she needs to start with a list of the most important questions, bearing in mind the relevance of the interview to the programme as a whole, and the amount of time it's likely to be on screen. Four is a reasonable number in most cases, but only the first one, which may also be introducing the interviewee, needs to be specified, and remembered, in full. The others can merely be prompts, because what the interviewer needs to do is phrase the next question so that it leads logically from what the interviewee has just been saying.

This is very much a knack which improves with practice. Another is the ability to decide when a supplementary question is needed, either to draw the interviewee out to finish his story, or to follow up a new and promising angle on what he or she is saying. But it's a question of balancing the value of the new material against the danger of the interview being sidetracked, or running on too long for its place in the finished programme.

One point which *must* be borne in mind, though, when drawing up the questions is to persuade the interviewee to answer in the form of statements rather than single words. It helps if none of the questions will allow the answer 'Yes' or 'No'. The old journalist's maxim of asking only those questions which start with words like who, why, when, where, what and how is a useful trick to use when drawing up an interview script. Other techniques can be picked up from watching television interviews with a critical eye — notice how many interviewers invite their respondents to 'tell' them about a specific part of the story, for example.

All these points apply whether you're recording an interview in a studio, or out on location against the background of the subject of the interview itself. But the trend with interviews on location is to avoid the sitting-in-two-chairs setup, and to go instead for interviews on the move — either walking through the interviewee's home town or place of work, or in his car driving to a location which plays a part in the programme itself. These are worth considering as a way of avoiding the interview slowing down the pace of the programme, but they do need special care, and a little pre-planning.

For a walking interview, try to pick a location where the surface is smooth and unobtrusive, since the camera operator (you!) will have to walk backwards in front of both the interviewer and interviewee. Because this is going to call for some skill in keeping the picture steady, practise the routine first; you'll find it's easier to stay in medium shot with both people in the frame. If you try to tighten in close on the interviewee, the inevitable camera movements will be more obtrusive.

As this is a fairly tiring technique, keep the camera going to record all the sound, but break up the sequence as far as you can. Move further ahead of the pair to capture the occasional long shot (useful as a cutaway because you can't see lip movements in detail). If you've time to use a tripod, then you can zoom in to a close-up of the interviewee. Let them walk past you out of shot now and again, and shoot them from behind as a visual break; another useful all-purpose cutaway. Other cutaways include close-ups of the two pairs of walking feet — shoot these on the end of a zoom, from the tripod, or walk behind them, carrying the camera at just below knee-level as you follow your two subjects with as steady a pace and as smooth a movement as possible.

Interviewing someone in a car is, in many ways, easier since everyone is at least sitting down. In this case, assuming the interviewee is driving, shoot from the front passenger seat with, if possible, the interviewee talking either directly to camera or just to the right of the camera — even though the questions are actually being asked from the back seat. When it's time to shoot the questions and the noddies, camera operator and interviewer change places. For cutaways, use shots of the interviewee's hands on the steering wheel or changing gear, their eyes as seen in the driving mirror (change the angle to make this possible), or shots of the traffic and surroundings outside — followed by a selection of passing shots of the car taken from roadside camera positions.

Finally, let's look a little more closely at the technique for vox-pop interviews. Assuming you want to record the views of a varied sample of the local people on (to return to the restored railway example) 'What do you think of the railway coming back to life?', then all you need do is record your presenter, or a voice-over commentator saying the question once only.

Once the introduction has been shot, in whatever form you see it, you're then free to shoot as many vox-pop responses to that question as you want. But it makes for more picture variety if you shoot them alternately to left of frame and to right of frame. You can also vary the background, if time and space allow, but it's more important that they face in alternate directions, since they're the main focus of interest in each case. If you *can* see much of the background behind them, try to make sure it's clearly part of the place we've just been looking at, as a reminder that the interviews were conducted on the spot, and didn't relate to some other location altogether.

The routine is much the same in each case. Place your subject in front of the right background, and looking to whichever side of the camera is appropriate. Explain to them the question you're going to ask, and the fact that you want a short, simple answer

Figure 46. Whenever you shoot people in close-up — for interviews or 'vox-pop' quotes, keep an eye on the background.

— something preferably longer than a 'yes' or 'no', but not a long and rambling paragraph saying the same thing at much greater length. Frame the picture as you want it, moving the contributor to left or right to avoid placing them against trees or telephone poles, then set the camera up in the 'pause' mode. Give them a rehearsal if it makes them feel less nervous. (Some professional cameramen and directors offer a dry run to nervous contributors and then shoot it anyway, since they're likely to be much less nervous if they think the camera isn't turning.) Then ask the question, press the start button and off you go.

There's no need for shots of the interviewer, or of any 'noddies', in this kind of mass interview. If you want to ask other questions, then bring the interviewer in to ask them to camera, or in voice-over, and then follow the question with a set of replies. But if anyone doesn't work as a contributor, either on a single take, or throughout, then treat it as a mistake. Go back on the tape to the end of the previous contribution, and start again with another take. Sometimes people will become less nervous with repetition, but sometimes their nervousness will increase to the point where there's no purpose in continuing, and you'd be well advised to thank them politely and move on to the next contributor. If you do, don't forget to record the new contribution over the last take of the previous one, and record them in the same position, otherwise your alternate left-right framing sequence will be disturbed.

Two more points which are worth making about interviews, or indeed any contributions from the public in programmes, both professional and amateur. These kinds of pictures are called 'talking heads', and it can be wise to be careful about how many of them you use. It all depends on how interesting they are. Sometimes people have so interesting a story to tell that you could have a half-hour programme of nothing but someone's reminiscences; but that kind of quality is rare. Sometimes you may have a succession of vox-pop interviews, candid expressions of what real people (rather than people working to a script) feel about the subject. Sometimes their interest is in the fact that the feelings they portray are unanimous, although their diversity is what makes them worth recording. As always, be on the lookout for how your audience is likely to feel — and if you feel the talking heads are taking over the programme then cut them down, or alternatively, look for cutaways and overlay shots of whatever it is they're actually talking about.

CHAPTER ELEVEN

THE SCRIPT

Trying to tell someone how to write a script for a television programme is a little like trying to tell them how to shoot it. Every programme and every subject ever made calls for a different way of approaching the script, and trying to cover a range of different approaches and treatments would end up only scratching the surface of the subject at one extreme, and creating a deep sense of confusion at the other, through simply trying to cover too much ground.

So we shall approach the subject in a similar way to the advice given earlier on shooting. A set of general guidelines, which should help you decide what your script should be doing and how it should be doing it — followed by an illustration of how the script would work in the example we used earlier, the controversy over the restoration of railway services in a local community.

DEFINING THE SCRIPT

First of all, though, it's essential to agree on what we mean by a script. To make a complex programme, there has to be a whole series of scripts. There's a dialogue script, for any dramatised sequences in the programme, there's the presenter's script to tell him what he has to say to camera, and when he has to say it, there's a sound script to lay down all the details of how the different soundtracks are to be mixed and balanced to make the finished programme sound-track. Then there are interview scripts to set out the questions to be put to the contributors and, once the interviews have been recorded, the quotes which will be used out of the answers they gave to those questions. There will also be a commentary script, for the voice-over which will be recorded onto the edited programme and, since professional programmes are very rarely shot in the same order as they're edited, there will be a shooting script to tell the production crew, the artists and the director the order in which the different shots will actually be recorded. Finally, there's the programme script which will tie all these different bits of information together as the master specification to which the programme will actually be made.

For many people, producing the script is the most daunting part of making a video programme. Something about the very idea of scriptwriting makes it sound challenging and dramatic — the kind of image which conjures up Scott Fitzgerald or Dennis Potter, turning out a masterpiece for the large or small screen. But that's like saying all cars are Rolls Royces, or all paintings are Picassos. Every programme ever made had to have a script; the script might exist on the back of an envelope, on a laundry bill or entirely in the producer's head, but the truth remains that precious few programmes would ever be completed unless someone, somewhere, had an idea of what it was trying to say, and how it was going to try to say it.

So let's approach this matter of scriptwriting, as we've tried to approach every other part of the art of programme-making so far; let's follow the professionals in how they approach their tasks, but let's keep it simple in keeping with our objectives. As with everything else, once you've proved you can write a simple script or make a simple programme, developing your ideas and your techniques so that you can turn out work which is more ambitious and more successful is much less daunting a prospect.

In our case we're going to begin with the programme script, as that's the most important document of them all. It's the script with most relevance to the editing stage, which is the final step in producing the finished programme, and it's also the most complete of the scripts. As we just mentioned, most of the other scripts are obtained from it, either by taking extracts from it in certain specialised areas

— like the interviews or the commentary — or by rearranging the information it contains — as in the shooting script.

The first stage involves going back to the treatment, which set out to define the story in outline. You may remember that the treatment itself defined the order in which sequences and sections of the programme would be put together, and this provides the outline framework of the script itself. But remember also that the treatment could, and probably did, change and develop as research and shooting progressed. Nearly every production involves a difference between what was originally planned, in terms of shooting and interviews, and what was actually recorded, and the last and final version of the treatment should reflect that.

So, the final version of the treatment gives us the skeleton for the script. Writing the script effectively involves putting flesh on the bones it provides; turning the notes in the right-hand column into the words which your presenter and voice-over commentary will say. The sequence notes in the left-hand column can also be expanded into a full list of the shots you'll be using in the programme, as this information will be needed for the editing stage. If the treatment you're working from has been put together properly, writing the script itself is something you may find surprisingly straightforward, provided you remember two priorities.

SCRIPTING YOUR COMMENTARY

The first requirement is clarity, and the second is simplicity. Remember that your audience is not going to be reading your words, or the words of any of your contributors — they're going to be hearing them. Keep the sentences short, keep the words and phrases simple, let the pictures tell the story. Don't tell the audience about what they can already see for themselves on the screen — use the commentary to tell them all the background facts which the pictures can't convey.

It's a useful idea to read out the words you've written for the commentary. You don't want a breathless commentary from the start of the programme to the finish without a break. Establish a gentler pace, with room for the action and the sound effects to help the story along on their own. Some scriptwriters say a ratio of about two minutes of words to every three minutes of programme is the right kind of ratio to aim at, but this will probably vary a little from subject to subject.

So far, we've been talking about subjects which are scripted before they're shot. In that sense, the job of the script is to tell your audience about the subject you've chosen in the same way as you might tell them yourself, face to face. Just as appearing in front of the camera requires that you treat it as a friend to be informed and entertained, so your script should treat the audience in the same way. Surprise them, inform them, entertain them — as clearly and as economically as you can, reinforcing the pictures and the messages *they* carry rather than repeating them in words. Learn to think in terms of picture sequences to match the words you give your presenter or your commentary — work to a treatment which sets out what the programme will do, in words or pictures, from start to finish.

But be careful never to become the slave of your script. No matter how carefully you research the subject, no matter how often you visit the locations before shooting begins, and no matter how long you spend talking to contributors before you interview them, there are *always* surprises waiting once you start to make your programme. Be flexible, and learn to respond to changes by changing your script, and your approach, where necessary. Learn to see surprises, not as hostile events which undo your careful preparation, but as opportunities to make an even better programme. In a documentary, a new shift in the subject can make your programme more topical — in a drama, a change of weather or in a location may give you the chance to take advantage of it, to build it into the story in some way.

Figure 47. Make every shot justify its place in your sequence. If a shot is static, like this one, only use it if it actually makes a point — the immaculately restored booking office in a railway station, the calm before the afternoon rush — which can be emphasised, if necessary, in your voice-over commentary.

Now let's go back to our railway story. We looked at three different ways of treating the opening sequence, so perhaps the most straightforward example we can take at this point is a little further into the programme, where we want to show how popular the service has become with visitors. Assume we shot a sequence of three shots in the station booking office; the queue of people lining up outside to wait for tickets, the clerk taking the money and stamping the tickets, and then the crowds waiting on the platform outside, as seen through the booking-office window.

The first question to ask yourself is 'What's unusual about what we're seeing?' It isn't people paying money for train tickets, nor people queuing to hand over their money at that. It isn't the crowds on the platforms either — it's the combination of all these things with the holiday clothes and atmosphere. So what we need is something along the lines of:

'What is it that makes people queue up to hand over hard-earned money for a ride on a train? Not to get to work, not to make some urgent and special journey to the other end of the country — but just as a way of spending a pleasant holiday afternoon with the rest of the family'. That commentary amounts to a total of 57 words — just about right for the first section, covering the subject of the shots in the right order.

Now to the second section. Here again, we have three shots — the coaches waiting at the platform with people climbing aboard, the engine backing onto the head of the train, and a panning shot up to the crest on the side of the tender. The sequence lasts for just 22 seconds — equivalent to between 55 and 66 words of script. So here goes, once again: 'It's certainly a popular idea — there's precious few seats to spare on any of the trains *(over the crowded coaches in the platform)*. But no-one seems to mind, for this is a very different kind of railway — it's privately run, and all the trains are hauled by beautifully restored steam engines *(over the engine backing onto the train)*. It's a colourful trip back into the past, and it's absolutely nothing to do with British Rail . . .' *(Pan to the old railway's crest on the tender, emphasising the lack of connection with British Rail)*. The total — 62 words — is once again the right kind of length to do justice to the pictures.

On now to the third sequence in this section of the script — an interview with the shopkeeper who says his trade has been ruined by the crowds and traffic resulting from the reopening of the line. We have a shot of him adjusting the display outside his shop which lasts six seconds, before we go into his response to the first question of his interview which is: 'What difference has the return of the railway made to you?' All that is needed for the link is something along the lines of: 'But not everyone sees the return of the railway as a blessing. Whitchurch shopkeeper Joe Bloggs . . .' That's enough to bridge the gap into his reply to the unspoken question, which fits neatly on the end.

In one way scriptwriting becomes a little like trying to solve a crossword puzzle, finding words to suit the pictures and to fit into specified gaps. It means everything has to be timed to the pictures — or the pictures have to be timed, in some cases like interviews, around the spoken word. And although it can become fascinating to listen to, you need to incorporate sections of the programme where the pictures and sound effects can tell the story on their own, allowing the script to breathe and providing a much-needed gap in the commentary.

SCRIPTING THE UNPREDICTABLE

Of course, some programmes can't *start* with a script in this way. Treatments which depend on actual events being recorded as accurately as possible may not be predictable enough for a full script to begin with. In those cases, produce as flexible a treatment as you can from the research you've been able to do — even if you don't know exactly how a contest or event will finish, you must know what you want your programme to say, and this must influence how you approach the programme. So work out what parts of the subject you will be shooting, in which order, and then keep your eyes open for any change in circumstances which may mean a new angle. Once the programme is shot, you can then write the script, safe in the knowledge that all you now have to do is explain what the audience won't know from simply watching the pictures.

It's difficult to think of enough examples to cover all the different kinds of programme subject which fall into this category. One possibility might be some local sporting derby between two neighbouring villages — say, a cricket match or a tug-of-war — where the history of previous events in the series has established a clear favourite and an equally clear outsider. Your finished script will obviously depend on who finally wins the contest you're shooting —so you can't write it beforehand. All you can do is postpone the creative decisions which depend on which team wins, until you actually know.

So the treatment might be drawn up with a look at both villages, and a few vox-pop interviews about the importance (or the irrelevance) of the event to most of the inhabitants. Then you could look at some of the more interesting characters from both teams, at their backgrounds, at what they feel about the contest, and about their opponents. By the time the event is ready to begin, you can select your shots to heighten the drama of the contest, by looking for anything which suggests that *this* year, perhaps, the outsiders will overturn the predictions being made. Whichever way the result eventually goes, the will-they-won't-they quality of a possible victory against the odds is bound to hold your audience's interest.

This quality can be heightened afterwards, when you *do* write the script in the light of the final result. On the day, your priorities are to capture anything which stresses the closeness of the contest, the anxiety of the competitors, and the possibility that either side may win. The longer the result is in doubt, the better for your programme — from your point of view, the worst possible result is an early victory for the favourites.

If this should happen have a contingency plan ready. Make the most of the early stages of the contest. Capture the announcement of the result, and then concentrate on the emotions of the losers. Why *do* they feel the event is so predictable? Could their approach to the contest be at fault? What are they going to do to make next year a different story, and so on. On the other hand, if the outsiders *do* win, then some of those questions will need to be put to the losing favourites, in between concentrating on the joy and surprise of the victory. Ask some of the experts why this change in fortunes happened this year. And after it's all over, ask the inhabitants of the winning village whether they now feel the same about the event as before.

Depending on the outcome of the contest, you will now end up with a finished programme, apart from the script. Your audience will see two villages,

Figure 48. Covering a sporting event, like a dragon boat race, means shooting the action as it happens. Only before and after the event can you shoot interviews or comments which can be edited into the sequence as cutaways, or used as voice-over comments where they relate to the action being shown in the picture.

interviews with people in the villages, interviews with people preparing for a sporting event, shots of the event itself, with one team being announced as the winner, wild jubilation on one side and disappointment on the other, then some more interviews to round the whole thing off. All that's needed is an explanation of where we are, what's happening and who's talking — and there's your script.

CHAPTER TWELVE

EDITING

So far, most of the different skills and techniques of programme-making we have covered in the book have been based fairly closely on those used by professional television producers and their teams. Until recently, though, there was one fundamental exception: editing. Where the amateur programme-maker was largely limited to assembling a programme shot by shot, in the order in which his camcorder recorded them, the professionals had infinitely greater freedom. They were able to perform the video equivalent of putting a cine film together — cutting, trimming and splicing together shots from different locations and different days, in a different order, with maximum flexibility in how they assembled the finished programme from the material they had amassed, together with titles, graphics, special effects and a fully mixed soundtrack.

THE EDITING REVOLUTION

The big difference, and the source of the problem, was that in video — as opposed to film — no cutting or splicing actually takes place. What happens instead is that each shot is copied from the tape on which it was recorded while shooting, onto a master tape on which the programme is built up from all the different inputs. And instead of the simple cutting-and-splicing equipment used for film editing, this calls for two (or more) recorders and a complex control unit to ensure that the right sections of each shot are copied and added at the right point on the master tape.

So one of the biggest revolutions in programme-making for the non-professional has been the opportunity to edit video properly. The previous generation of cameras suffered from the drawback

Figure 49. The power of creative editing: with a careful choice of subjects and a fade in and out between scenes, you can show in a few seconds a journey which may have taken several days to complete!

that each time the camera was switched on, it ran up to speed and commenced recording without automatically back-spacing and editing the new shot onto the tail end of the previous one. This meant that as shot succeeded shot on the tape, the boundary between each new shot and the previous one tended to be very untidy.

In-camera (or more exactly, in-camcorder) editing changed all that. Because the camera took care to assemble-edit the new shot onto the existing one, a tape with a succession of different shots recorded on it did at least resemble a finished programme in that the cuts were clean and stable, and the picture material remained on screen, without any gaps, from start to finish. But the biggest restriction, from the creative point of view, was that assembling a programme meant shooting every shot in the order in which it was needed. Not only that, but it was essential for each shot to start precisely as the camera started recording. If the action being recorded was a second or two late getting under way, then the pause had to be accepted, or the shot had to be re-recorded — and, furthermore, the tape had to be wound back to the starting point of the shot being replaced.

Paradoxically, this made programme-making for the amateur enthusiast far more difficult and time-consuming than it was for his professional counter-part, because it was necessary to edit the programme on the shoot itself. Only when another step forward in equipment capability made it possible to record an insert edit (a shot recorded earlier in a pre-assembled sequence to cover an existing shot — in some cases with, in others without, altering the sound) was part of the tyranny of the what-you-shoot-is-what-you-get limitation of earlier cam-corders broken. But even that meant the editing had to be done on location, since the insert shot had to be edited in place by recording it at the time.

The third step in the editing revolution came with the option of editing back at base. This can be done by linking the camcorder to the input of a VCR, so that tapes loaded into the camcorder (containing footage recorded on it previously) can be copied shot by shot onto a programme master tape loaded in the VCR. It's still a fairly laborious process, because the input tape(s) have to be loaded one by one into the camcorder and played back through the viewfinder until the right start point appears and the 'pause' button is pressed. As the editing takes place, shot by shot, you can watch each shot being copied across on a TV set connected to the output of the VCR. When you reach the end-point of the shot (allowing an overlap safety margin), you then pause the tapes, and look for the next shot in the sequence, which could be on the same camcorder tape, or on another tape altogether.

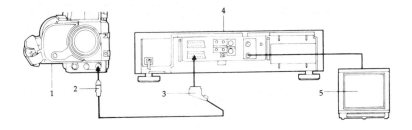

Figure 50. A home-video editing setup, using the camcorder (1) connected to the back of a VCR (4) via a lead sporting compatible connectors (2 and 3). The programme is built up shot by shot on a tape contained in the VCR. Each new shot is identified on the tape on which it was first recorded, copied across to the VCR and viewed on the TV (5).

But the latest home-video technology, though more expensive, has much more in common with profes-sional editing equipment. It takes the form of a control unit which is introduced in between the camcorder and the VCR (or even two VCRs). In some cases, special circuits arrange the output signal so that the input tape is seen on one half of the screen of the TV connected to the output VCR, alongside the image of the picture on the output tape. This allows the editor to search through the input tape(s) quickly to find the shot which is needed, identify the edit points using the control unit, and even to preview the edit so it's possible to assess the match between the shots before actually recording onto the programme master tape.

THE FREEDOM FACTOR

So much for what the equipment can do — how should it be used to edit your programme together?

Once again, as with shooting and scripting, it's impossible to give a long list of hard and fast rules to suit every situation. The most important advantage of this kind of edit capability is that it frees your creative ideas far beyond the bounds of having to shoot material in order, and it puts you on a similar footing to all other film and programme makers.

Let's look at a couple of examples of the difference which after-the-event editing can make. In the case of an event like a motor-race meeting, or a day at a horse-racing track, you have the freedom to concentrate on one particular target at a time. Because each event will usually consist of a series of races, spread out through the day, you can plan your shooting to make the most of that timetable. You can shoot your crowd shots during the first race, for example. You can shoot the preparations for a race later in the afternoon before a different one altogether, you can capture the action of the racing in later races (provided the details coincide sufficiently to make the illusion convincing) and you can use the final race of the day to capture the spectators' reactions to the result. That's a fairly logical shooting order, in that it still follows chronologically the order of events on the day — but if you wanted to shoot the sequences in an entirely different order, then there's nothing to stop you. It can all be built up into a coherent and entertaining sequence at the editing stage, even if it was all shot in the most confusing and contradictory order possible.

This same freedom applies to other subjects, and to individual sequences too. For the railway programme we looked at earlier, you could take time to travel on one of the trains from one end of the line to the other. The editing facility allows you to intercut this passenger's-eye view of moving countryside as a visual punctuation wherever you need one, right through the programme. You could also do the opposite, pick up a shot of a passing train whenever the time allows, then use the edit facility to bring all these passing shots in together to create a vivid and varied sequence of trains at work.

There are all kinds of ways in which the variable timescale, which can be created through careful editing, will work for you in heightening the creativity of your programmes. Take the family's wedding video, for example. How much more variety could you put into the programme if you shot some of the frantic rehearsals and preparations, the inevitable crises and problems which arose and were solved along the way, and edited them in as a series of flashbacks on the record of the day itself? Or this year's family holiday could be contrasted with the holiday last year, or the year before, or some of the ideas and expectations which people harboured beforehand, could be contrasted with whether they actually measured up to the reality, as captured by your camcorder. In fact, it's impossible to think of any subject matter where the ability to edit in total freedom won't make a powerful difference to the creativity, the impact and the entertainment value of the finished programme.

ACQUIRING THE TECHNIQUE

There is one proviso, though. Editing *is* a skill, which needs to be learned through practice as much as through following a set of strict and definite rules, laid down in advance and which cannot be broken at any price. The golden rule, when editing one shot onto the end of another is, if the cut looks right, then it *is* right. Only if the cut looks ugly, or clumsy, or abrupt, or confusing is it better to cut at a different point instead.

A good rule is always to try to cut out of a shot as soon as you feel it has lasted long enough — far more shots look wrong because they last too long, than because they're too short. But don't cut on the middle of a sharp movement, since that can suggest a too-abrupt cut to the audience, which will have been expecting to see the end of the movement before the cut. On the other hand, if you have deliberately planned for a cut on that movement, and have shot the same person making the same movement from a different camera position, then cutting from one shot to the other in the middle of the movement can be a very attractive cut indeed — provided you've shot enough overlap to give you a choice of exactly where you make the transition between one shot and the other, and provided the continuity matches in all other respects, that is.

A useful general rule is to try to time your cuts so that the main focus of interest in a picture — the brightest colour or the most obvious movement — is in a similar part of the screen in the shot which follows it. That way, the audience's concentration will be led smoothly from one picture to the next without being distracted by the cut. If, on the other hand, the subject of both shots is the same, then try to make sure the subject is a different size in the frame. And always, always, *always* avoid jump-cuts like the plague!

You also need to be careful with camera movements. It's better not to cut when the camera is in the middle of a zoom or a pan (unless the movement is *very* slow). On the other hand, you can sometimes cut a shot to avoid movement, by editing to another just before you reach a point where the camera wobbles or shakes. When you *do* use a zoom or pan shot, put enough of the shot on to establish the picture before the movement actually starts — often half a second is enough — otherwise the cut may look hurried by comparison with the pace of the pictures up to that point. But don't leave it too long, as that may suggest that the camera operator was late on cue with the movement.

When you cut interviews, you can go through the recorded material and limit yourself to the strongest answers. You can usually cut the first, introductory question, and put it in the voice-over commentary instead, so the interview really starts with the first response from the interviewee. You can then cut back to the interviewer for each of his or her questions, and to a 'noddy' of the interviewer whenever you want to bridge a troublesome gap in the interviewee's answers.

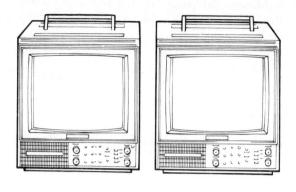

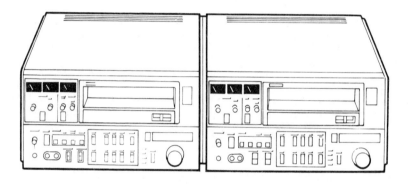

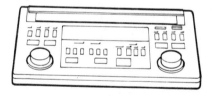

Figure 51. The professional equivalent of the home-editing setup in the previous drawing. This is a basic two-machine edit suite, with the original shots being played on the left-hand machine and watched on the left-hand monitor. They are copied, using the control unit at the bottom, onto the programme tape contained in the right-hand machine, and watched on the right-hand monitor. More complex edits involving mixes and more ambitious special effects may use two, three or more input machines to build up the sequence on the master tape machine.

Although video editing allows you to shoot the material in whatever order you like, it *does* impose one discipline. Because it's a copying process, rather than the physical cutting and splicing of film editing, it does usually have to be done in order. The editor starts at the beginning of the programme and carries on building it up, shot by shot, until the end is reached. This makes it difficult to shorten or lengthen shots in the middle of the programme once the edit is complete, as can easily be done in film editing (unless you re-edit everything following the changed shot). Video editing therefore has to be much more precise from the beginning. Only when the editing is finished can the voice-over commentary be added — and if any sections don't fit the edited pictures, then the script itself will have to be modified to fit.

The best way to do this is to produce a shot list of the finished, edited programme. This will list the edit shot by shot, with the subject of the shot and its exact duration. Interview sections and presenter-to-camera sequences can be summarised as a single entry in each case, as no script needs to be written and recorded to cover them — likewise sections of the programme to be covered by music, or by sound effects, alone or in combination. Once the shot list is complete, the voice-over script can be checked against it, on the basis of two-and-a-half to three words per second, to make sure the words suit the picture sequences without too much of a struggle. It's also important to be sure that a reference to a particular subject occurs when that subject is actually on the screen, and that voice-over sections end in time for presenter sequences or interviews to start with a suitable pause. If not, then the script needs modifying, often by a word here or a phrase there, until the sound fits the pictures perfectly. Then you can record it, and use the edit equipment to dub it onto the soundtrack of your programme master tape section by section — and then your programme is virtually complete.

Of course, there's now an ever-widening choice of equipment reaching the home video market to make this final post-production stage even more ambitious; audio mixers to produce a professional balance between words, sound effects and music, graphics generators to produce captions and credit titles, and special-effects generators which can dissolve or wipe between one shot and the next. These can all be useful — dissolves in particular can be invaluable in marking a transition between one sequence and another, in suggesting the passing of time or even (sparingly) in avoiding an ugly cut. But like all special effects, they need planning, and often recording, before they can be used in the edit.

In fact, so much has happened, in terms of the complexity, variety and sheer sophistication of the equipment now available, that there is much less to separate the capabilities of the amateur programme-maker from his or her professional opposite numbers. But this only serves to make the creative element of your programmes even more important — not to make up for the shortcomings of the equipment, but to capitalise to the full on all its capabilities. That, in a nutshell, is the purpose of this book: to show you the ropes, and suggest some initial ideas and ways of thinking. That's all any book can hope to do, without an overload of detail. For the next step has to be practice, as much practice as possible, in order to sharpen the impact and entertainment value of the programmes you make to fully professional standards. By picking simple subjects and simple treatments to begin with, but by disciplining yourself in planning and shooting, you'll find your skill and experience grow with each new assignment. In a very short time, you'll find your programmes improving out of all recognition — which, in the end, has to be the greatest compensation, and the greatest enjoyment, of all.

INDEX

Figures in italics refer to illustrations.